The Peace Movement

Nancy Harris, *Book Editor*

Bruce Glassman, *Vice President*
Bonnie Szumski, *Publisher*
Helen Cothran, *Managing Editor*

GREENHAVEN PRESS
An imprint of Thomson Gale, a part of The Thomson Corporation

THOMSON
━━━━━★━━━━━ ™
GALE

Detroit • New York • San Francisco • San Diego • New Haven, Conn.
Waterville, Maine • London • Munich

LIBRARY OF CONGRESS CATALOGING-IN-PUBLICATION DATA

The peace movement / Nancy Harris, book editor.
    p. cm. — (At issue)
  Includes bibliographical references and index.
    ISBN 0-7377-2431-5 (pbk. : alk. paper) — ISBN 0-7377-2430-7 (lib. : alk. paper)
    1. Peace movements. I. Harris, Nancy. II. At issue (San Diego, Calif.)
  JZ5574.P43 2005
  303.6'6—dc22   2004040268

Printed in the United States of America

Contents

Introduction

Prior to the U.S. invasion of Iraq in 2003, Stephen Downs, a sixty-year-old lawyer, was arrested at a shopping mall in New York. Downs, who was wearing a T-shirt with the message "GIVE PEACE A CHANCE" on the front and "PEACE ON EARTH" on the back, was asked by guards to leave the mall, but he refused to comply. The guards left and returned with police officers who repeated the request. When Downs again refused, the police arrested him for trespassing. When questioned about the incident, a mall executive initially said that Downs had been disruptive but later admitted that the messages on his T-shirt had prompted the lawyer's arrest. Incidents such as this one became more prevalent as the United States moved toward a war with Iraq, reflecting a growing tension in the country between antiwar protesters and supporters of President George W. Bush's policies in the war on terrorism.

In the tense months following the September 11, 2001, terrorist attacks on the World Trade Center in New York City and the Pentagon in Washington, D.C., the initial shock, horror, and grief felt by Americans were followed by feelings of fear and wariness. In his response to the September 11 terrorist attacks, President Bush declared a war on terrorism. In an address to Congress and the American public on September 20, 2001, President Bush stated, "Either you are with us or you are with the terrorists." The U.S. government then began its efforts to track and eradicate worldwide terrorism. It began with an attack on Afghanistan, which at that time was ruled by the Taliban, a fundamentalist Islamic militia that had given refuge to al Qaeda, the Islamic terrorist group believed to have orchestrated the attacks on the United States. Although the U.S. military successfully deposed the Taliban and many al Qaeda members were killed or captured, military forces were unable to apprehend al Qaeda leader Osama bin Laden. Months later, the Bush administration broadened its war on terrorism to include threats of a war against the Saddam Hussein regime in Iraq. On the home front, the administration responded to terrorism with the creation of the Department of Homeland Security and the passage of the USA PATRIOT Act, an effort to unite and strengthen America by providing law enforcement tools to intercept, deter, and punish terrorist acts against Americans in the United States and around the world.

Peace activists' responses

Peace activists reacted negatively to both the possible war with Iraq and to the Patriot Act. While the war on Afghanistan had broad support, the war on Iraq was more controversial, leading to more protests and breathing new life into the peace movement. Peace activists believed a war with Iraq was unjustified, that no evidence had ever been found to link al Qaeda with Saddam Hussein in Iraq, and that America's leaders had questionable motives for wanting to attack Iraq. Educator and editor Barbara Epstein states,

> Most of the people who became involved in the antiwar movement did so out of their conviction that the international ambitions of the Bush administration endanger peace, democratic rights, and prosperity in the United States and abroad. It is taken for granted, in the antiwar movement, that the Bush administration wants both oil and power, and that the close relationship between the Bush administration and the oil companies is a factor in the administration's actions.

Peace activists also felt that the Patriot Act was a mistake because it allowed random searches, unwarranted seizures, and arbitrary arrests not only of potential terrorists, but of innocent civilians as well. In addition, the act created a public climate of tentativeness and reticence, stifling dissent and limiting freedom of speech.

To make their opinion heard, peace activists spoke out against war, using the Internet as a tool for organizing and communicating. The largest antiwar demonstrations in history were held worldwide.

Criticism of the peace movement

By contrast, Americans who strongly supported President Bush and an attack on Iraq thought peace movement activists were unrealistic and naive and that the peace movement's message of "no war" offered no alternative for fighting terrorism. Pro-war advocates also believed that peace activists were unsympathetic to the Iraqi people who were suffering under the tyranny of a cruel dictator, Saddam Hussein. Polls indicated that a majority of Americans supported the president and war in Iraq. For many Americans, patriotism meant love and devotion to America and support for the president. Because peace activists did not support going to war with Iraq, they were seen as unpatriotic and anti-American. Author and right-wing activist David Horowitz described the antiwar protesters as "hate-American radicals" akin to the leftists who supported totalitarian movements during the Cold War. In his words, "The hate America left is attempting to silence right-thinking citizens. It is attempting to divide the home front in the face of the enemy. Even as we go to war."

The suppression of dissent

Because peace activists were seen as anti-American, they encountered an active resistance to their protests by law enforcement officers, the media, and other Americans. For example, on October 24, 2003, at an airport in Columbia, South Carolina, where President Bush's plane was scheduled to land, activist coalition director Brett Burnsey raised a sign in the airport crowd that read "NO WAR FOR OIL." Police ordered Burnsey to leave the area. When Burnsey asked why the people with pro-Bush signs were not being asked to leave, the police informed him that the message on his sign was the reason. Police told Burnsey to move to a "free-speech zone" a mile from the airport. When Burnsey was arrested for refusing to move, he faced federal charges and a possible six-month prison term.

In addition, celebrities who spoke out against the war were condemned on television and on radio stations for using their status to promote their antiwar agendas. When Natalie Maines, the lead singer of the country music band the Dixie Chicks, spoke out against President Bush, her band's music was banned on some radio stations. As actor Tim Robbins stated, "If you oppose this administration, there can and will be ramifications. Every day the airwaves are filled with warnings, veiled and unveiled threats, spewed invective and hatred directed at any voice of dissent."

On some college campuses, antiwar protesters met strong reactions. A Yale woman received rape and death threats following the publication of an antiwar article she had written for the campus paper. Negative response to the peace movement caused people around the country to remove antiwar bumper stickers in fear of vandalism. Military wives who questioned the necessity of the war in Iraq, where their husbands were deployed, became reluctant to express their opposition for fear of damaging their husbands' careers.

In response to charges that they are unpatriotic, many peace activists defend their patriotism. As stated by journalist and peace activist Rebecca Solnit, "We were not against the US and for Iraq; we were against war, and many of us were against all war, all weapons of mass destruction—even ours—and all violence everywhere. We are not just an antiwar movement. We are a peace movement." Peace activists believe that war in the Middle East will further threaten the United States by provoking more terrorist activity. Furthermore, peace activists feel that the freedom to voice their views is at the core of what it means to be American. They believe that a true democracy depends upon the free expression of differing points of view to create a society that is vital and dynamic.

The peace movement was unable to stop the war in Iraq. However, as the example of Stephen Downs illustrates, the movement brought to light underlying tensions, provoked debate, and stimulated ideas about what could be done to strengthen the peace movement. In *At Issue: The Peace Movement*, authors debate the effectiveness of the peace movement, its tactics and philosophies, and its prospects for achieving its goal of a nonviolent world.

1

The Movement Against the Iraq War Was a Failure

Nathan Newman

Nathan Newman is a union lawyer and vice president of the National Lawyers Guild. He is a community activist and technology analyst who has written for several journals including MIT's Technology Review. *Newman is the author of* Net Loss, *a book on Internet policy and economic inequality.*

The movement against the 2003 war in Iraq failed due to the movement's lack of organization and lack of a plan to help Saddam Hussein's resisters in Iraq. The antiwar movement did not do the work necessary to support their position in comparison to the prowar contingent who spent years publishing books and holding conferences in support of military action. Consequently, the movement's message of "no war" was too simplistic and offered nothing in place of military aggression. The broad democratic left is responsible for the peace movement's failure, as well as for the failure of the antiwar rallies where speakers preached to the already converted and did nothing to lessen support for the Iraq war. The left should have done more outreach to the undecided.

When U.S. Troops entered Baghdad, I was very glad to see the pictures of Iraqis celebrating freedom from Saddam's dictatorship. Not because they changed my view that the war was wrong, but because they meant that for some Iraqis the

Nathan Newman, "Where the Peace Movement Went Wrong," *Dissent*, vol. 150, Summer 2003, p. 12. Copyright © 2003 by Dissent Publishing Corporation. Reproduced by permission.

death and devastation of the war would be off-set by their freedom from Saddam's yoke.

The problem for the peace movement is that its activists failed to argue persuasively that war was not the best way to achieve this goal, leaving many Americans with the sense that the choice was between fighting and doing nothing—which ended up tilting moderates reluctantly toward the war camp. For them, the war involved fighting a brutal regime that abused its own people and invaded its neighbors. That the Bush leadership had other, nastier intentions is another question—since progressive people could see the Bush administration doing the right thing for the wrong reasons. So the antiwar argument had to be about alternative ways to achieve the goal of a freer and more democratic Iraq—and about the unlikelihood that Bush and Co. would actually do that.

The "no war" message was too simplistic

The antiwar movement lost the argument on the efficacy of alternative means partly because of its simplistic choice of "no war" unity over a more sophisticated and positive message—which also would have required more outreach to people who don't go to rallies (and probably less focus on rallies). And when we allowed groups such as the Workers World Party, which had defended the Hussein regime in the past, to lead some of the antiwar rallies, many folks might rightly have thought that such a movement had no real plan to challenge Saddam's regime.

If we want to oppose war effectively, we need to provide a far clearer roadmap showing how we plan to support those who resist oppression. Mouthing lines about national sovereighty in cases like Iraq is as hollow as Bull Connor's[1] using states rights rhetoric to justify keeping the National Guard out of the South. There is absolutely nothing wrong with humanitarian intervention in principle. What should be opposed is the use of military force when nonviolent solidarity is more likely to lead to a just result and to impose much lower costs on the population. But in the case of Iraq, the lack of an articulated plan to help those resisting Hussein is exactly what strength-

1. Eugene "Bull" Connor was the commissioner for public safety in Birmingham, Alabama, during the 1960s. He brutally opposed segregation on the grounds of states' rights.

ened the argument of the hawks that their method was the only way to "liberate" Iraq. There was no counter-argument from the antiwar movement about how it was acting, or could or would act, in solidarity with the oppressed people of Iraq. That was the fatal flaw of antiwar organizing.

The left cannot plead lack of time, because it had all the time necessary between the first and Second Gulf Wars to mount a public education campaign in defense of Kurdish and Shia human rights and for nonviolent strategies that could have served as an effective alternative to war. It was the first Bush administration that sold out both the Kurds and the Shias when they rose up in 1991, yet the left failed to rally to their support.

That was a substantial reason why many liberals moved into a position of support for the war. You can say they were all misinformed by the media, but in January and February of [2003], only about one-third of the American public supported war without significant global support, as signified by UN endorsement, whereas by March and April an additional 40 percent supported Bush's unilateral intervention. It was the failure of the antiwar forces to hold that 40 percent that needs to be analyzed.

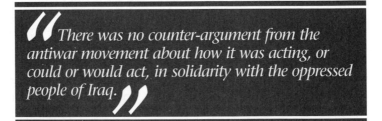

There was no counter-argument from the antiwar movement about how it was acting, or could or would act, in solidarity with the oppressed people of Iraq.

The neoconservatives had been doing their intellectual outreach for years, publishing books, holding policy conferences, organizing at the grassroots to solidify an ostensibly moral basis for their position, while the left was largely throwing its critique together on the fly.

The left was flatly outorganized on this issue, not because it had fewer resources but because its activists just didn't do the work necessary for a serious intellectual engagement. Failing that, the only "unity" position possible was the simplistic "no war" message, and anyone, including pro-Hussein propagandists, could speak in the name of the antiwar movement. The message was too thin, and it failed.

Democratic left responsible for failure

The broader democratic left is responsible for that failure: its myriad groups and endless divisions means that it cannot sustain the solidarity necessary over the long haul to debate and develop a positive political strategy. There is too much self-indulgence, too many ego-driven and fundraising-driven organizational divisions, too many tiny groups without the needed heft for long-term organizing. There is no space where the millions of people who rallied against the war ever have a chance to participate beyond showing up at a rally.

> *There should have been broader mass outreach to the unconverted middle, whether door-to-door, going to community meetings, or just talking on street corners to those who would listen.*

With no long-term alliances to develop a coherent strategy and no groups with a mass of members, we end up at any moment of crisis depending on the usual list of famous names and obscure grouplets to legitimatize and organize our efforts. This ad hoc method of operating leads to little more than agreeing on NO as the only message. And that's not enough.

Bits and pieces of a more sophisticated response to the war, moral and political, appeared sporadically at antiwar rallies, but they were marginal to the simplistic "no war" legalisms and "unity" rhetoric. Speakers at the rallies I went to were preaching to the converted, not to those who were unconvinced of Bush's complete perfidy and for whom an actual argument was necessary.

The antiwar movement was a failure. Many of my left friends will point to the "success" of the large rallies, but what's the achievement? Rallies are means, not ends. Why should we praise tactics that coincided with an increase in support for unilateral war?

Broader outreach needed

There should have been broader mass outreach to the unconverted middle, whether door-to-door, going to community meetings, or just talking on street corners to those who would listen. Although there was some impressive Internet outreach by groups such as MoveOn.org and some broader outreach by select groups, the overall de-emphasis on door knocking and the attached organizing is the exact problem with the strategy of much of the antiwar left that preferred to talk to itself at rallies or in its existing media circle.

Things need to change, and quickly. We might start by concentrating on working to guarantee that the Iraqi people get the democracy they have been promised, keep control of their oil resources, and escape their country's debt (much of which is owed to the Western governments and companies that armed the military we just fought). The left needs a positive agenda, not merely a defensive NO as its reflexive organizing response.

More broadly, we need a global message of solidarity with all who are experiencing oppression and human rights violations, whether by governments allied to the United States or by governments opposing it. We need a clear moral message, for in a world where the U.S. military has demonstrated that no military force can oppose it, only a cohesive global movement exerting clear moral force will be able to defeat Bush's unilateralism.

Despite the shift of public opinion toward the pro-war position once the war started, the earlier opposition to unilateral war making shows that there is fertile ground for organizing among the broad public, in the United States and abroad. But the democratic left still needs to build the right kind of organizations and develop the right message to reach them.

2

The Movement Against the Iraq War Was a Success

Ibrahim Ramey

Ibrahim Ramey is the director of the Peace and Disarmament Program at the Fellowship of Reconciliation in New York. He is an advocate for just U.S. policies and cofounded the Campaign of Conscience, an organization that sponsored a nationwide effort to lift the nonmilitary sanctions on the people of Iraq. Ramey is a board member of the Central Committee for Conscientious Objectors and the Muslim Peace Fellowship. He has spoken and led workshops worldwide on social justice and community organizing.

As the United States dropped bombs on Iraq, it was evident that the peace movement was not a failure and that it was not defeated. This conclusion is supported by the magnitude of the antiwar demonstrations against the Iraq war and points to the emergence of a new global majority against war. This majority reaches across a vast social spectrum, including ordinary, nonpolitical individuals, organizations, many religious communities, and organized labor. The peace movement demonstrated a clear moral position against Iraq's governmental policies and the prowar "right" was never able to portray the protesters as supporters of Saddam Hussein. In addition, the strong divisiveness and contradictions among top U.S. military leaders helped promote the peace movement's position. Although the peace movement's position did not keep the United States from declaring war on Iraq, it is important for peace activists to remember that the war system is immense and may take decades to overcome.

The government of the United States is at war with Iraq. Despite the heroic efforts of the UN Security Council and the overwhelming evidence of a desire for peace displayed by literally millions of anti-war protesters in over 60 countries, President Bush and his junior partner in crime, Tony Blair, have deployed military forces and launched a ferocious attack against Saddam Hussein and, more importantly, the people of Iraq.

As the cruise missiles and bombs fall on Basrah and Baghdad, some cynics and skeptics are pronouncing the death of the peace movement (along with the virtual demise of the UN as a relevant institution). They—the war hawks, the unilateralists and the supporters of Mr. Bush—say that we have failed.

Evidence of success

Here are a few reasons why we have not:

1. The sheer magnitude of the ongoing demonstrations against this war signifies the emergence of a new "global majority" against war. Millions—perhaps tens of millions—of demonstrators, from Melbourne to Miami, from New York to New Zealand, from the developing world to the metropoles of Europe and North America, have rejected the rush to war and affirmed the legitimacy of international law and its primary global proponent, the United Nations. The world has, quite literally, not seen this powerful a consensus for peace since the protests against the U.S. in Viet Nam in the 60's and 70's.

2. The consensus against military action is far bigger than just the "peace movement" and the "Left." True, much of the energy to mobilize demonstrations, civil disobedience and other forms of dissent came from the traditional anti-war and left-of-center formations that traditionally criticize US foreign policy and the war system.

But hundreds of nonviolent actions against the rush to war also came from ordinary, non-political organizations and individuals more localed in the political "center," and especially from those who had no history of radical organizing or taking part in protest politics. It showed that vast numbers of people—across the entire political spectrum—were outraged over the plan (now operational) to invade and conquer Iraq.

3. The movement against war clearly articulated that it was

not a movement to support the regime of Saddam Hussein. Unlike the Vietnam-era activists, who were often mis-characterized as ideological tools of the Viet Cong and the North Vietnamese, the anti-Iraq war movement demonstrated, overwhelmingly, a clear moral position against both US government and Iraqi government policies. Opposition to the war against the Iraqi people was never confused with support for the dictatorship that oppresses them, and the pro-war "Right" was never able to (falsely) portray the anti-war movement as apologists for Saddam.

> *The sheer magnitude of the ongoing demonstrations against this war signifies the emergence of a new 'global majority' against war.*

4. This time, the religious communities and organized labor were largely with us, and they were with us early on. Faith communities and unions came out against the Bush administration war plans in large numbers, despite the retreat and collapse of the traditional Democratic Party "opposition" that was too cowed by the false prowar consensus presented by the "Right." It's significant to also note that numerous mainstream religious leaders—including Pope John Paul II—were unwavering in their pronouncements of the immorality of the military attack on Iraq.

5. The drive to war exposed major divisions and contradictions within the US military itself. The cabal of Donald Rumsfeld, Richard Perle, Paul Wolfowitz, and other cold-war hawks might have won the battle to initiate the war, but they did so with significant (and public) opposition from figures like Generals Norman Schwartzkopf and Anthony Zinni, both respected, high-visibility figures in the military establishment who publicly criticized the pro-war hype and constantly asserted the position that Iraq (even in light of Iraq's possible possession of banned weapons) did not constitute a threat to the security of the United States.

6. The racist nature of the war against the Iraqi people has been exposed. A broad cross-section of Third World communities and leaders from multiple social sectors (labor, religion, elected officials, women's organizations, youth) has been a vig-

orous and growing component of the anti-war movement both in the USA and internationally. Black leaders and activists alike have vehemently denounced the twisted budget priorities that siphon hundreds of billions of dollars from vital human needs to the war machine. In fact, according to national news polls, only 35% of the African-American public supports the war, significantly less than the reported majority of whites.

Continue the pressure

So members, don't get weary.

War against Iraq may have begun, and war is always a tragedy. But in times of crisis, we should remember that war is a system, not an event, and that challenging a system as immense as the war system involves a protracted struggle that will take decades to win. And even while war rages on, we can—and must—continue to pressure the US government to both limit (and end) the military aggression and assume its moral responsibility to the Iraqi victims of the violence. And we should not forget our responsibility to the thousands of US service personnel who will return from this conflict, possibly disillusioned and traumatized, or seriously ill from exposure to depleted uranium (now in use) and other "mysterious" ailments sure to emerge in the aftermath of Gulf War II.

We are not defeated at all. If anything, this movement against war in Iraq has demonstrated the power of a broad, democratic human community opposed to war, and the immense gulf between this majority community and the minority circles of the government, the Pentagon and the corporate profiteers that promote the war system to the detriment of the rest of us.

One more thing. Waging war is, ultimately, a political act that requires state political power. Bush and his friends may have it now. But they are not guaranteed to have it forever.

We should continue to declare that this war is not in our name and it will not be fought with our consent. It is immoral, illegal and illegitimate.

3

Peace Activists Must Demand Nuclear Disarmament and Work Actively for Peace

Dennis Kucinich

Dennis Kucinich is a U.S. representative from Ohio and a progressive Democrat who ran in the 2004 presidential race. He formerly served as mayor of Cleveland, Ohio, as well as a state senator. He is chairman of the Congressional Progressive Caucus and is a human rights and environmental activist. Kucinich advocates a Department of Peace and is the recipient of the 2003 Gandhi Peace Award.

In the expanding "war on terrorism," the Bush administration has suggested the use of nuclear weapons, making the issue of nuclear disarmament vitally important. To practice nuclear disarmament, the United States must abide by the principles of the Nuclear Nonproliferation Treaty, revive the Anti-Ballistic Missile Treaty, and prohibit the introduction of weapons into space. In addition, Americans must speak out against nuclear weapons, against the idea that war is inevitable, and against all barriers to the creation of a peaceful world.

> "Come my friends, 'tis not too late to seek a newer world," . . . Alfred Lord Tennyson

If you believe that humanity has a higher destiny, if you believe we can evolve, and become better than we are; if you

Dennis Kucinich, "Peace and Nuclear Disarmament: A Call to Action," www.WagingPeace.org, March 2002. Copyright © 2002 by the Nuclear Age Peace Foundation. Reproduced by permission.

believe we can overcome the scourge of war and someday fulfill the dream of harmony and peace on earth, let us begin the conversation today. Let us exchange our ideas. Let us plan together, act together and create peace together. This is a call for common sense, for peaceful, non-violent citizen action to protect our precious world from widening war and from stumbling into a nuclear catastrophe.

> **❝ We should speak out and caution leaders who generate fear through talk of the endless war or the final conflict. ❞**

The climate for conflict has intensified, with the struggle between Pakistan and India, the China-Taiwan tug of war, and the increased bloodshed between Israel and the Palestinians. United States' troop deployments in the Philippines, Yemen, Georgia, Colombia and Indonesia create new possibilities for expanded war. An invasion of Iraq is planned. The recent disclosure that Russia, China, Iraq, Iran, Syria, North Korea, and Libya are considered by the United States as possible targets for nuclear attack catalyzes potential conflicts everywhere.

These crucial political decisions promoting increased military actions, plus a new nuclear first-use policy, are occurring without the consent of the American people, without public debate, without public hearings, without public votes. The President is taking Congress's approval of responding to the Sept. 11 terrorists as a license to flirt with nuclear war.

Going to war is a political decision

"Politics ought to stay out of fighting a war," the President has been quoted as saying on March 13th 2002. Yet Article 1, Section 8 of the United States Constitution explicitly requires that Congress take responsibility when it comes to declaring war. This President is very popular, according to the polls. But polls are not a substitute for democratic process. Attributing a negative connotation here to politics or dismissing constitutionally mandated congressional oversight belies reality: Spending $400 billion a year for defense is a political decision. Committing troops abroad is a political decision. War is a political decision. When men and women die on the battlefield that is the result of a political decision. The use of nuclear weapons, which can end the lives of millions, is a profound political decision. In a monarchy there need be no political decisions. In a democracy, all decisions are political, in that they derive from the consent of the governed.

In a democracy, budgetary, military and national objectives must be subordinate to the political process. Before we celebrate an imperial presidency, let it be said that the lack of free and open political process, the lack of free and open political debate, and the lack of free and open political dissent can be fatal in a democracy.

We have reached a moment in our country's history where it is urgent that people everywhere speak out as president of his or her own life, to protect the peace of the nation and world within and without. We should speak out and caution leaders who generate fear through talk of the endless war or the final conflict. We should appeal to our leaders to consider that their own bellicose thoughts, words and deeds are reshaping consciousness and can have an adverse effect on our nation. Because when one person thinks: fight! he or she finds a fight. One faction thinks: war! and starts a war. One nation thinks: nuclear! and approaches the abyss. And what of one nation which thinks peace, and seeks peace?

> *This is a call to action: to replace expanded war with expanded peace. This is a call for action to place the very survival of this planet on the agenda of all people, everywhere.*

Neither individuals nor nations exist in a vacuum, which is why we have a serious responsibility for each other in this world. It is also urgent that we find those places of war in our own lives, and begin healing the world through healing ourselves. Each of us is a citizen of a common planet, bound to a common destiny. So connected are we, that each of us has the power to be the eyes of the world, the voice of the world, the conscience of the world, or the end of the world. And as each one of us chooses, so becomes the world.

Each of us is architect of this world. Our thoughts, the concepts. Our words, the designs. Our deeds, the bricks and mortar of our daily lives. Which is why we should always take care to regard the power of our thoughts and words, and the commands they send into action through time and space.

Possibility of nuclear war

Some of our leaders have been thinking and talking about nuclear war. In [March 2002] there has been much news about a planning document which describes how and when America might wage nuclear war. The Nuclear Posture Review recently released to the media by the government:

1. Assumes that the United States has the right to launch a pre-emptive nuclear strike.

2. Equates nuclear weapons with conventional weapons.

3. Attempts to minimize the consequences of the use of nuclear weapons.

4. Promotes nuclear response to a chemical or biological attack.

Some dismiss this review as routine government planning. But it becomes ominous when taken in the context of a war on terrorism which keeps expanding its boundaries, rhetorically and literally. The President equates the "war on terrorism" with World War II. He expresses a desire to have the nuclear option "on the table." He unilaterally withdraws from the ABM [Anti-Ballistic Missile] treaty. He seeks $8.9 billion to fund deployment of a missile shield. He institutes, without congressional knowledge, a shadow government in a bunker outside our nation's Capitol. He tries to pass off as arms reduction, the storage of, instead of the elimination of, nuclear weapons.

> **"** *This is the time to conceive of peace as not simply being the absence of violence, but the active presence of the capacity for a higher evolution of human awareness.* **"**

Two generations ago we lived with nuclear nightmares. We feared and hated the Russians who feared and hated us. We feared and hated the "godless, atheistic" communists. In our schools, we dutifully put our head between our legs and practiced duck-and-cover drills. In our nightmares, we saw the long, slow arc of a Soviet missile flash into our very neighborhood. We got down on our knees and prayed for peace. We surveyed, wide eyed, pictures of the destruction of Nagasaki and Hiroshima. We supported the elimination of all nuclear weapons. We knew that if you "nuked" others you "nuked" yourself.

Dichotomized thinking

The splitting of the atom for destructive purposes admits a split consciousness, the compartmentalized thinking of Us vs. Them, the dichotomized thinking, which spawns polarity and leads to war. The proposed use of nuclear weapons, pollutes the psyche with the arrogance of infinite power. It creates delusions of domination of matter and space. It is dehumanizing through its calculations of mass casualties. We must overcome doomthinkers and sayers who invite a world descending, disintegrating into a nuclear disaster. With a world at risk, we must find the bombs in our own lives and disarm them. We must listen to that quiet inner voice which counsels that the survival of all is achieved through the unity of all.

We must overcome our fear of each other, by seeking out the humanity within each of us. The human heart contains every possibility of race, creed, language, religion, and politics. We are one in our commonalities. Must we always fear our differences? We can overcome our fears by not feeding our fears with more war and nuclear confrontations. We must ask our leaders to unify us in courage.

We need to create a new, clear vision of a world as one. A new, clear vision of people working out their differences peacefully. A new, clear vision with the teaching of nonviolence, nonviolent intervention, and mediation. A new, clear vision where people can live in harmony within their families, their communities and within themselves. A new clear vision of peaceful coexistence in a world of tolerance.

What the United States must do

At this moment of peril we must move away from fear's paralysis. This is a call to action: to replace expanded war with expanded peace. This is a call for action to place the very survival of this planet on the agenda of all people, everywhere. As citizens of a common planet, we have an obligation to ourselves and our posterity. We must demand that our nation and all nations put down the nuclear sword. We must demand that our nation and all nations:

- Abide by the principles of the Nuclear Non-Proliferation Treaty.
- Stop the development of new nuclear weapons.
- Take all nuclear weapons systems off alert.
- Persist towards total, worldwide elimination of all nuclear weapons.

Our nation must:

- Revive the Anti-Ballistic Missile treaty.
- Sign and enforce the Comprehensive Test Ban Treaty.
- Abandon plans to build a so-called missile shield.
- Prohibit the introduction of weapons into outer space.

We are in a climate where people expect debate within our two party system to produce policy alternatives. However both major political parties have fallen short. People who ask "Where is the Democratic Party?" and expect to hear debate may be disappointed. When peace is not on the agenda of our political parties or our governments then it must be the work and the duty of each citizen of the world. This is the time to organize for peace. This is the time for new thinking. This is the time to conceive of peace as not simply being the absence of violence, but the active presence of the capacity for a higher evolution of human awareness. This is the time to conceive of peace as respect, trust, and integrity. This is the time to tap the infinite capabilities of humanity to transform consciousness which compels violence at personal, group, national or international levels. This is the time to develop a new compassion for others and ourselves.

When terrorists threaten our security, we must enforce the law and bring terrorists to justice within our system of constitutional justice, without undermining the very civil liberties which permits our democracy to breathe. Our own instinct for life, which inspires our breath and informs our pulse, excites our capacity to reason. Which is why we must pay attention when we sense a threat to survival.

Challenges that threaten the planet

That is why we must speak out now to protect this nation, all nations, and the entire planet and:

- Challenge those who believe that war is inevitable.

- Challenge those who believe in a nuclear right.
- Challenge those who would build new nuclear weapons.
- Challenge those who seek nuclear re-armament.
- Challenge those who seek nuclear escalation.
- Challenge those who would make of any nation a nuclear target.
- Challenge those who would threaten to use nuclear weapons against civilian populations.
- Challenge those who would break nuclear treaties.
- Challenge those who think and think about nuclear weapons, to think about peace.

It is practical to work for peace. I speak of peace and diplomacy not just for the sake of peace itself. But, for practical reasons, we must work for peace as a means of achieving permanent security. It is similarly practical to work for total nuclear disarmament, particularly when nuclear arms do not even come close to addressing the real security problems which confront our nation, witness the events of September 11, 2001.

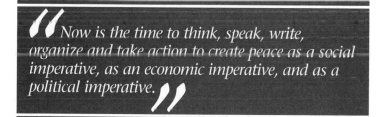

Now is the time to think, speak, write, organize and take action to create peace as a social imperative, as an economic imperative, and as a political imperative.

We can make war archaic. Skeptics may dismiss the possibility that a nation which spends $400 billion a year for military purposes can somehow convert swords into plowshares. Yet the very founding and the history of this country demonstrates the creative possibilities of America. We are a nation which is known for realizing impossible dreams. Ours is a nation which in its second century abolished slavery, which many at the time considered impossible. Ours is a nation where women won the right to vote, which many at the time considered impossible. Ours is a nation which institutionalized the civil rights movement, which many at the time considered impossible. If we have the courage to claim peace, with the passion, the emotion and the integrity with which we have claimed independence, freedom and equality we can become that nation which makes non-violence an organizing principle in our society, and in doing so change the world.

Create a Department of Peace

That is the purpose of HR 2459. It is a bill to create a Department of Peace. It envisions new structures to help create peace in our homes, in our families, in our schools, in our neighborhoods, in our cities, and in our nation. It aspires to create conditions for peace within and to create conditions for peace worldwide. It considers the conditions which cause people to become the terrorists of the future, issues of poverty, scarcity and exploitation. It is practical to make outer space safe from weapons, so that humanity can continue to pursue a destiny among the stars. HR 3616 seeks to ban weapons in space, to keep the stars a place of dreams, of new possibilities, of transcendence.

We can achieve this practical vision of peace, if we are ready to work for it. People worldwide need to be met with like-minded people, about peace and nuclear disarmament, now.

- People worldwide need to gather in peace, now.
- People worldwide need to march and to pray for peace, now.
- People worldwide need to be connecting with each other on the web, for peace, now.

A world wide web forum for peace

We are in a new era of electronic democracy, where the world wide web, numerous web sites and bulletin boards enable new organizations, exercising freedom of speech, freedom of assembly, freedom of association, to spring into being instantly. Thespiritoffreedom.com is such a web site. It is dedicated to becoming an electronic forum for peace, for sustainability, for renewal and for revitalization. It is a forum which strives for the restoration of a sense of community through the empowerment of self, through commitment of self to the lives of others, to the life of the community, to the life of the nation, to the life of the world.

Where war making is profoundly uncreative in its destruction, peacemaking can be deeply creative. We need to communicate with each other the ways in which we work in our communities to make this a more peaceful world. I welcome your ideas at dkucinich@aol.com or at www.thespiritoffreedom.com. We can share our thoughts and discuss ways in which we have brought or will bring them into action.

Now is the time to think, to take action and use our talents and abilities to create peace:

- in our families.
- in our block clubs.
- in our neighborhoods.
- in our places of worship.
- in our schools and universities.
- in our labor halls.
- in our parent-teacher organizations.

Now is the time to think, speak, write, organize and take action to create peace as a social imperative, as an economic imperative, and as a political imperative. Now is the time to think, speak, write, organize, march, rally, hold vigils and take other nonviolent action to create peace in our cities, in our nation and in the world. And as the hymn says, "Let there be peace on earth and let it begin with me."

Nuclear disarmament and peace are possible

This is the work of the human family, of people all over the world demanding that governments and non-governmental actors alike put down their nuclear weapons. This is the work of the human family, responding in this moment of crisis to protect our nation, this planet and all life within it. We can achieve both nuclear disarmament and peace. As we understand that all people of the world are interconnected, we can achieve both nuclear disarmament and peace. We can accomplish this through upholding an holistic vision where the claims of all living beings to the right of survival are recognized. We can achieve both nuclear disarmament and peace through being a living testament to a Human Rights Covenant where each person on this planet is entitled to a life where he or she may consciously evolve in mind, body and spirit.

Nuclear disarmament and peace are the signposts toward the uplift path of an even brighter human condition wherein we can through our conscious efforts evolve and reestablish the context of our existence from peril to peace, from revolution to evolution. Think peace. Speak peace. Act peace. Peace.

4

The Peace Movement Is Naive

Adam G. Mersereau

Adam G. Mersereau is an attorney in Atlanta, Georgia. He served in the U.S. Marine Corps from 1990 to 1995.

Peace is a state that exists only between wars. The United States and the rest of the world are faced with a new threat of terrorism, a new kind of senseless killing and destructive warfare. Negotiations, economic sanctions, and appeasement are useless in the face of this new threat. Peace activists are naive to think that their passive messages for peace will stand up to this threat. Many peace activists adhere to a form of utopianism that holds that the human race is evolving toward a higher plane of existence and that humans are basically good. In the minds of these peace activists, it is wrong not to give dictators such as Iraqi leader Saddam Hussein a chance to show their goodness. This kind of thinking shows that peace activists are naive and unrealistic, which makes them more helpful to America's enemies than to America.

Editor's Note: The following article was published two months prior to the start of the U.S. war in Iraq in 2003.

The advocates of "peace at any price" are not waiting for a declaration of war against Iraq. Months ago they booked flights and hotel rooms and scheduled time off from work and school to attend prewar protests in America and abroad. Many have spent hours kneeling over posters with wide-tipped magic markers, scratching out their signature policy proverbs, such as "CHOOSE PEACE NOT WAR." An activist group called Voices in the Wilderness is sending small groups of American and British protesters to Baghdad. Over 100 celebrities signed an open letter opposing military action in Iraq. In October [2002] actor Sean Penn placed an ad in the *Washington Post* that criticized President Bush's war policy. He then traveled to Baghdad to assess the situation for himself and, presumably, for his fans. Not surprisingly, Mr. Penn concluded that America, not Iraq, is to blame for the current tensions between the two nations. No doubt he will trek to Pyongyang . . . and reach a similar conclusion.

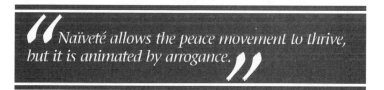

Naïveté allows the peace movement to thrive, but it is animated by arrogance.

Peace activists may be well intentioned; but at their worst, they are more helpful to America's enemies than to America. The best we can say is that they are clinically naïve. They are as insufferable as a college freshman who believes he and his political-science professor can end poverty if only people would listen. It is as if the peace activists believe they have discovered for the first time those self-evident and those ancient truths that human life is sacred, and war is tragic. Little do they know that a majority of the Iraqis who stroll past their peace marches in Baghdad support an American invasion. Many would eagerly fight and risk death in an armed revolution if they could obtain the resources and momentum to launch one for themselves.

Naïveté allows the peace movement to thrive, but it is animated by arrogance.

The arrogance

While campaigning for the presidency, candidate Bush said that his administration would conduct its foreign policy with less arrogance than past administrations had displayed. He is now widely accused of forsaking the less-arrogant approach and of choosing, instead, to rattle his saber at any dictator he thinks he can rattle. But is it really arrogant for the president to insist that a violent and unpredictable dictator with ambitions to control the world's oil supply—who is also a friend of al Qaeda—should be denied a secret nuclear, chemical- and biological-weapons program? Is it arrogant to suggest that Saddam Hussein [former leader of Iraq] should be removed from power if he continues to defy and deceive the international community? Likewise, is it arrogant to expect the North Koreans to abide by the Agreed Framework, under which the U.S. promised to inject millions of U.S. tax dollars into the faltering North Korean economy? Perhaps it is slightly arrogant, but the peace movement is fantastically more arrogant.

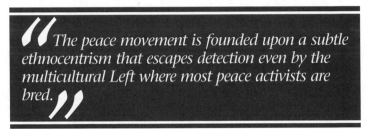

The peace movement is founded upon a subtle ethnocentrism that escapes detection even by the multicultural Left where most peace activists are bred.

The peace movement is founded upon a subtle ethnocentrism that escapes detection even by the multicultural Left where most peace activists are bred. The group that most openly celebrates the diversity of mankind does not understand that many people in the world hold diverse beliefs and subscribe to ideologies that are entirely independent of American influence. In the mind of the peace activist, America is not just the sole superpower, it is the center of gravity for all world events; and so every world event is simply an equal (and sometimes opposite) reaction to a prior American action. Peace activists believe that America's economy and culture are such dominant forces in the lives of people throughout the world that the actions and policies of other nations can be interpreted only as mere reactions to the actions and policies of the United States government. Therefore, they believe America has the unbounded ability to manipulate foreign governments through economic and cultural means.

Peacenik foreign policy

Peacenik foreign policy is really very simple: Without an action by the United States, there will be no reaction by others. If America does not start a war, there will be no war. This is the arrogant ethnocentrism of the peace movement. Under this view, it is unthinkable that quaint little dictators—such as Saddam

Hussein or Kim Jong-il [leader of North Korea]—might deign to manipulate America as much or more than America tries to manipulate them. It is unthinkable that a nation would resort to building nuclear weapons if they did not first feel threatened by the world's only super-bully. It is inconceivable that Saddam Hussein or Kim Jong-il might have diabolical plans and evil aspirations that were not created by, and are not controlled by, the U.S. State Department. The peace activist then reaches the conclusion that the United States can make a unilateral decision for peace, simply by choosing to lay down its arms. If the United States would ignore open and notorious breaches of U.N. directives and treaties, and simply refuse to disturb the current state of peace, then peace would prevail by default.

Of course, the choice between war and peace is not ours alone. There could be war—and likely will be war—regardless of our course of action. The only questions are: on whose terms, and on whose turf?

More evil than war . . . is the sentiment that pervades the peace movement: That there is nothing worth fighting for.

Many members of the peace movement also hold tightly to a loosely defined utopianism. They believe that the human race (save conservative Republicans) is evolving toward a higher and more noble plane of social existence. The activists themselves are, of course, at the forefront of the evolutionary curve; while the Cro-Magnon in the White House and his Cabinet of Neanderthals stubbornly resist progress. Although the Left has largely declared the concepts of "good" and "evil" to be passé, the peace activist believes that the heart of man is intrinsically "good," and that it would be "evil" if we do not give Saddam Hussein every chance to let his goodness shine through.

Utopianism is dead in the minds of most people, because as veterans of the 20th century, which was the bloodiest century ever, we cannot deny that "good" and "evil" are entangled within the hearts of men and many of his ideologies, and that peace is little more than a welcome respite between wars. We also know that unless the Saddam Hussein's and Kim Jong-il's of the world are Utopians too, then to champion utopianism in America or Europe is useless. Utopianism is folly; unilateral utopianism is suicidal. But rather than adjust their policy to reflect reality, the peace activists will march in circles, carry their signs, and wait for reality to reflect their policy.

Trouble in utopia

While the peace activists march, the president and his Cabinet must face reality. Nations acquire weapons of mass destruction for one of three reasons: to deter their enemies, to obtain leverage in diplomacy, or to attack. Nations that wish to accomplish either of the first two objectives must announce their arsenals to the world. America is open about its nuclear capabilities to deter aggression. North Korea has boldly announced its nuclear capacity to set up another diplomatic shakedown. A nation keeps its weapons program secret, conversely, if it is planning an attack. Iraq's weapons program is highly secretive.

Iraq also has ties to a terrorist network that is unlike any of America's historical enemies. The man who recently sprayed bullets into a Southern Baptist hospital in Yemen, killing three American missionaries and wounding a fourth, confessed that he did it to "get closer to God." Negotiations, economic sanctions and even appeasement are useless in the face of this new threat: terror as an end in itself. The peace activists have nothing to offer toward a solution. They are wrong to distinguish between the war on terror and the war against Iraq. Terrorists need money, safe harbor, weapons, training and intelligence. All signs indicate that al Qaeda gets them from sponsor states such as Iraq. Again, the peace activists have no response other than "CHOOSE PEACE NOT WAR."

The peace activists are sincere, dedicated, and sometimes they display bravery and even a patriotism of sorts. But their policy of unilateral passivity will leave us vulnerable to being nickeled-to-death. Jimmy Carter was right when he said that war is evil, but only in the sense that war is the most undesirable state of human affairs. More evil than war, however, is the sentiment that pervades the peace movement: That there is nothing worth fighting for. Luckily there is a large group of Americans—those in uniform—who are willing to do the very dirty work that may be necessary to achieve another extended period of peace.

5

The Peace Movement Is Counterproductive

Nicole Banda

Nicole Banda is a student at Cornell University who writes for the Cornell Review, *the school's conservative newspaper.*

Antiwar protesters did not make coherent arguments against the U.S. war with Iraq. Although protesters complained about the violence of war and the imperialistic motives of the United States, the protesters said nothing about the atrocities committed by Iraqi dictator Saddam Hussein, and they were unrealistic to think that Hussein could be peacefully reasoned with. It is the duty of the president and the American government to protect Americans against the threat posed by dictators such as Hussein.

Jane Marie Law, a professor of religious studies ardently opposed to our nation's war in Iraq, recently addressed a group of Cornellians, criticizing anti-war protestors lack of eloquence, she insisted that such empty slogans as "F—— Bush" (and I will include "Bush is not an emperor", "No blood for oil", "Drop acid, not bombs", "Bomb Israel", "Drop Bush, not bombs", etcetera) hardly help the liberal pacifists' case against war but only highlight their inability to form coherent arguments. Law went on to urge her fellow pacifists to learn the art of rhetoric already mastered by their conservative counterparts. The complaints expressed by Law are obviously shared by a number of conservatives who have resigned themselves to the Left's inability to argue effectively against the war, but it is indeed suprising, perhaps even encouraging, to hear the complaints launched against the anti-war protestors' unintelligible babble (respect-fully) by their own kind. One liberal Cornellian recently con-fided to me, "I don't want to agree with this war, but none of the liberal's arguments make any sense!" Similar complaints have been echoed throughout campus both by my own liberal friends and by strangers whose conversations just happened to float my way. At one recent anti-war rally, a friend related to me, every time he tried to challenge one protestor with a question, the pro-testor shouted, "No war in Iraq!"

Dissenters criticize war and violence

As the war is being waged, dissenters continue to express their disgust for America's actions, and their inadequacies do not end with their lack of eloquence. On the evening of March 24th, for instance, five female panelists sponsored by the Cor-nell Anti-War Coalition gave a discussion entitled "Women Against War" in which they highlighted the various ways that women emerge as the largest group victimized by war. A Cor-nell professor, Anna Marie Smith, admonished the "super-power bent on world domination . . . with an unprecedented bent on arrogance" and warned that the war will "rob femi-nism of conditions we need to succeed" (Condoleezza Rice [na-tional security adviser] apparently disagrees). Law professor Marcia Greenberg predicted "the invasion of Iraq will lead to the death of thousands of civilians", and Andrea Parrot focused on rape and sexual assault that occur during times of war fo-cusing on such cases as the Rwandan genocide in 1995 and the thousands of Muslim women raped in Serbian war camps. While their criticisms of war and violence were touching, it is remarkable that not one addressed the issue of the United States' security against the threat of a chemical (or nuclear)-empowered, America-hating, terrorist-supporting Saddam Hus-sein. Instead, they focused on the depravity of America: launching an "immoral campaign to impose its will", forcing women into the role of "the mistress of the plantation", "em-pire building", and marking "the end of the First Republic". Their complete disregard for the dire risks that confront Amer-icans and Iraqis alike while Saddam remains in power is shock-ing but remains a common thread in the anti-war movement.

These voices of opposition provide concrete evidence of the wave of idealism we see infiltrating the ranks of these protest-ing pacifists. Their disdain for violence and yearning for peace is commendable until it begins to threaten the safety of our nation. Were our president to heed their advice and do nothing allowing Saddam's quest for WMD [Weapons of Mass Destruction] to take its course, he would not be fulfilling his constitutional obligations to provide for the common defense. Despite the longing of multiculturalists to see the world as "one people", we cannot expect our leaders to view the world in the same light. The American government's duty is to protect Americans, even when other countries tell it not to, even when the very people it is trying to protect publicly denounce its efforts and liken its actions to Nazism. It is unfortunate that these protestors refuse to recognize the futility of peacefully reasoning with an ambitious and heartless dictator. (I'd like to call it girly, but I won't. I will say this—flowers and hugs would hardly have been effective against the likes of Hitler or Stalin.)

> *It is unfortunate that these protestors refuse to recognize the futility of peacefully reasoning with an ambitious and heartless dictator.*

Since the war has begun, the protestors have tried a new strategy, claiming they speak on behalf of the soldiers—"I support the troops, but I don't support the war" has become their latest rallying cry. But many people find it hypocritical that "America is not an empire" pins have suddenly been replaced by "Support our troops; bring them home". Cornellians who have watched their brothers, their lovers, and their friends bravely risk their lives for the safety of all Americans are grieved and angered at protestors' ungraciousness. As Marine Corps officer candidate Gabriel Ledeen stated to one such protestor:

"I find it disingenuous of you to claim that you support our troops now, when it is politically convenient to do so. Groups with which you identify have been railing against the military for years and years, idolizing those who burned down ROTC facilities. They spat on returning veterans in the '60s and early '70s. They have been protesting against the 'homophobic' and 'sexist' practices of the military, banning recruiters from career fairs all over the country, closing down ROTC units at Ivy League and other universities, campaigning against tax breaks for military families and against an increase in the shamefully low military salaries. It is convenient now to present your arguments within the framework of a pro-military view, since nobody would listen to you otherwise."

While their voices have been heard, the president certainly does not agree. And rather than channeling their energy into productive humanitarian action, they continue to march, continuously and rudely preventing the exchange of ideas. These are the people who threw fruit at a conservative Cornell alum as she addressed her alma mater, who bellowed and booed when Pat Buchanan rejected their ideas, and who tried to drown out speakers at the Support the Troops rally on March 26th in Ho Plaza with vulgar and offensive yells. (At the risk of comparing apples to oranges, when was the last time you saw an unruly group of conservatives on campus obliterating the efforts of liberals to be heard?) They conspire to prevent ordinary Americans from being able to work, drain the resources of our police and firefighters who are trying to protect us from another terrorist attack, destroy and disrupt as self-proclaimed "peacekeepers", and then wonder why we call them unpatriotic. Disruption and dissension are not inseparable.

The U.S. government must stand firm

In the meantime, our government must stand firm so that these protesting idealists can rant and rave without the aid of a gas mask or duct tape. Our government must stand firm because twenty-four million people have been living under the tyranny of a man who gassed thousands upon thousands of Kurdish dissenters, who cuts out the tongues of those who speak against his authority, who uses plastic shredders to destroy his people, numb to their screams of agony, who financially supports men as they deliberately pursue the deaths of innocent men, women, and children.

Anti-war protestors are bewildering for this blatant disregard of human life. Their "peacekeeping" efforts belie their utter lack of compassion for the American and the Iraqi people alike. Their signs vilify our president even as he tries to protect us, but none condemn an evil murderer with no conscience. Idealistic, yes. And as Dr. Bill Bennet [conservative author and advocate] put it, "There's nothing that has the power to immunize against thought so much as ideology—and if you're an ideologue, evidence doesn't matter."

6

The Peace Movement Defines Itself as Patriotic

Patrick G. Coy, Gregory M. Maney, and Lynne M. Woehrle

Patrick G. Coy is associate professor at the Center for Applied Conflict Management at Kent State University, Ohio, and is editor of the annual volume Research in Social Movements, Conflicts and Change. *Gregory M. Maney is assistant professor of sociology at Hofstra University, New York. Lynne M. Woehrle is assistant professor of sociology in the Department of Behavioral Science and Social Work at Mount Mary College in Milwaukee.*

Following the September 11, 2001, terrorist attacks on the United States, peace movement organizations (PMOs) were in a difficult political climate. The government, mainstream media, and much of the general public argued that good patriotic citizenship meant supporting a retaliatory war against terrorists. The Bush administration took advantage of this climate by repeatedly using the media to enhance its prowar agenda. Consequently, peace movement organizations were challenged to redefine what patriotism meant in order to show that their pacifist activity was acceptably patriotic. As a result, some PMOs defined the core American values as truth, social justice, compassion, democracy, and a belief in the need for dissent. This strategy allowed PMOs to characterize opposition to war as a patriotic act.

In the days following the tragic events of September 11, U.S. peace movement organizations (PMOs) found themselves

Patrick G. Coy, Gregory M. Maney, and Lynne M. Woehrle, "Contesting Patriotism," *Peace Review*, vol. 15, 2003, p. 4. Copyright © 2003 by Taylor & Francis, Ltd. Reproduced by permission of the publisher and the authors.

operating in a difficult political climate. For the government, the mainstream media and the general public, "citizen," "patriot" and "retaliation" merged into a single "American" identity so that many felt that the nation and its way of life were at risk and that war was an appropriate response to the "new threat." Since then the mistaken hyperbole of an "everything has changed" approach to understanding September 11 has permeated most discussions of the event. While the extent of change is exaggerated, it is nonetheless true that significant shifts occurred in the political landscape in both domestic and foreign policy. In addition, relatively simplistic understandings of patriotism gained even more credence than usual in the U.S., and policy dissent was denigrated and more easily branded as unpatriotic.

'Loyalty to the Country Always; Loyalty to the Government When It Deserves It.'

A long-range and comparative approach to history shows that many of these political developments are predictable and relatively common when a state comes under attack on its home soil. But owing partly to the United States' placement as the world's lone military superpower and its imperial policies in a globalized economy, the attacks of September 11, 2001, also deeply influenced how Americans understand themselves and perceive their relationships to the rest of the world. For example, the false insularity that most Americans had long taken for granted was suddenly threatened. The Bush administration easily exploited this, rallying support for a policy of a permanent war economy, aggressive military retaliation, pre-emptive attacks abroad and civil liberty suppression at home. At the core was a call to intensely nationalistic patriotism.

Intense national pride

In a televised speech to a Joint Session of Congress, President Bush stated, "Tonight we are a country awakened to danger and called to defend freedom. Our grief has turned to anger, and anger to resolution. Whether we bring our enemies to justice, or bring justice to our enemies, justice will be done." In the same speech, the President praised Republicans and Democrats alike for singing "God Bless America" on the steps of the Capitol along with approving U.S. $40 billion to "rebuild our communities and meet the needs of our military."

The general public responded to the events of 9/11 with intense national pride. According to a study conducted after 9/11 by the National Opinion Research Center, 97 percent of respondents agreed "they would rather be Americans than citizens of any other country." The same study also offers evidence that elites successfully used this heightened nationalism to increase their own legitimacy. In the wake of the fiasco of the 2000 presidential election, public confidence in the executive branch of the Federal government had dropped to 13.5 percent. In the first survey taken after 9/11, confidence in the executive branch had risen to 51.5 percent. Confidence in the military nearly doubled from 39.7 percent prior to 9/11 to 77.4 percent afterwards. There was less room than ever for critical thinking about domestic and foreign policy decisions made by the power elites. Patriotism was over-simplified, as the "other" was made stark and dangerous.

> *Peace movement organizations constructed a notion of American identity that turned traditionally nationalistic themes into the service of peace, human rights and military moderation in the War on Terrorism.*

Given these changes, we set out to discover how American peace groups responded discursively to the challenges that 9/11 posed to their activism. We collected and coded official statements about September 11, 2001, the so-called "War on Terrorism" in Afghanistan and elsewhere, and the PATRIOT ACT from nine organizations: the American Friends Service Committee (AFSC); the Black Radical Congress (BRC); the Fellowship of Reconciliation (FOR); the New York Labor Coalition Against the War (NYLAW); Pax Christi (PaxC); Peace Action (PA); the War Resisters' League (WRL); Women's Action for New Directions (WAND); and the Women's International League for Peace and Freedom (WILPF).

Most of the 56 statements collected were issued between

September 11, 2001, and December 31, 2001. We defined "official statements" as press and media releases, printed statements, editorials and public calls to action from an organization's national office, issued in the name of the organization. These statements create a partial historical record of an organization's words and actions, and demonstrate how organizations contribute to discursive processes that shape the construction of patriotism.

Responding to hegemony

Peace movement organizations have at least two options in responding to the use of widely and deeply resonant cultural materials by power elites to secure mass consent to war (what Antonio Gramsci termed "hegemony"). On the one hand, they can create counter-cultures that directly challenge hegemonic concepts and practices. Norms that encourage deference to the state are questioned, resistance is celebrated and new practices are lived out.

Alternatively, groups can take a more complicated and subtler approach by employing cultural materials from the political mainstream that are likely to increase both bystander support and sympathetic media coverage by modifying, reclaiming or rewriting those materials. In this way, knowledge that is familiar and that resonates with a wide range of potential and actual constituents is turned to new purposes: the creation of oppositional knowledge that challenges government actions and supports political change. This oppositional knowledge may place pressure upon targeted elites to meet movement demands. We refer to this work by PMOs of co-opting symbols and meanings as "harnessing hegemony."

Our study suggests that peace activists both challenged hegemony and harnessed hegemony in the months following the September 11 attacks. For instance, one sign at a demonstration to protest the war in Afghanistan declared that "Patriots are Idiots: Matriarchy Now," while another read, "Loyalty to the Country Always; Loyalty to the Government When It Deserves It." The first directly challenges the conformist nationalist identity, suggesting that it uncritically accepts the *status quo* system of hierarchy, and calls for an alternative approach to power and order. In contrast, the second sloganeer harnesses patriotism, attempting to redirect its potency on behalf of the peace movement by decoupling the nation from the state.

Herein, we analyze the discursive techniques used by PMOs in their project of creating an alternative understanding of 9/11, the bombing of Afghanistan and the passing of the PATRIOT ACT. Overall, we found that the nine peace groups studied responded to the changed political landscape facing opposition movements in a post-9/11 United States by calling on bedrock American themes to critique the government's responses.

The true character of the United States

One area of discursive engagement was the role of September 11 in testing the United States' "true character" as a nation. In a televised address on the War on Terrorism, President Bush stated, "During the last two months, we have shown the world America is a great nation. Americans have responded magnificently, with courage and caring." The President went on to equate this true "American character" with the War on Terrorism. In contrast, peace groups claimed that opposing war was most consistent with the true character of America.

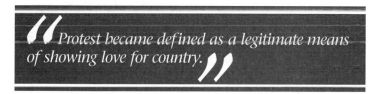

Protest became defined as a legitimate means of showing love for country.

Some of the organizations counseled that September 11 and the national crises it unleashed should be understood as a testing period, a "crucial moment" that created an opportunity for the U.S. to rely on its true values and to uphold its most deeply held constitutional principles. They clearly saw that the definition of what it meant to be an "American" was being contested. They also insisted that the stakes were even higher insofar as this was not just about how peace activists view themselves, but also about how others view them. For example, WILPF suggested that "the people of the world are watching" to see how the U.S. would respond, and counseled, "Let us demonstrate that our strength is in our resolve to maintain a democratic and free society and break the cycle of violence and retribution."

Similarly, Pax Christi issued statements designed to tap into reservoirs of relatively benign national pride by consistently calling forth from fellow citizens "the best of [the] U.S. tradition" and the "best of who we are." Pax Christi even drew upon maternal metaphors to inspire Americans to show their true character and honor traditional values through their opposition to retaliatory violence: "Our unspeakable grief and pain has, like a woman in labor, also given birth to a new sense of unity and has given the nation an opportunity to show its true character."

Harnessing the American identity

The usage of American identity themes was strongest in countering the war in Afghanistan. Peace movement organizations constructed a notion of American identity that turned traditionally nationalistic themes into the service of peace, human rights and military moderation in the War on Terrorism. For instance, while there was broad popular support in the United States for bombing Afghanistan and the larger effort to hunt for al-Qaeda members, AFSC, FOR, WILPF and PaxC each flatly rejected the equation of patriotism with support for U.S. policies and refused to join in the wave of blind patriotic nationalism.

For example, WILPF writing in response to the PATRIOT ACT and the U.S. intent to bomb Afghanistan suggested,

> We urge our fellow citizens to at least listen to those who, out of love of country, dare to say what many do not wish to hear. Our government, too, has in the past supported terrorists—including some of the very groups we fear today—and used the methods of terrorism to unseat democratically elected governments in the service of our own perceived "national interest."

The New York Labor Coalition Against the War harnessed American identity, proclaiming, "we are proud to be American trade unionists against the war," thus linking a traditionally pro-American image of the "trade unionist" to the anti-war movement.

Harnessing "American identity" thus redefined patriotism to mean dissent, including dissenting from a War on Terrorism that, while it may have had a just cause, was nonetheless being waged in an unjust manner, according to FOR. This was an important alternative in a political context described by FOR as leading "to an unquestioning patriotism that equates dissent with unAmericanism." Protest became defined as a legitimate means of showing love for country. Pax Christi tried to turn the tables on those who used patriotism to silence policy critics when it claimed that the highest form of patriotism is criticism itself: "There will be those who will try to tell us that criticizing our national policies in time of crisis is unpatriotic. But as William Fulbright, the former Senator from Arkansas reminds us, 'Criticism is more than right; it is an act of patriotism, a higher form of patriotism, I believe, than the familiar ritual of national adulation. All of us have the responsibility to act upon the higher patriotism which it to love our country less for what it is than for what we would like it to be.'"

Patriots uphold core values

Collective identities generally involve commitments to common principles. In the case of nationalism, patriots uphold the core values that unite the nation. In trying to mobilize the American public to support the War on Terrorism, President Bush sought to heighten patriotism by vilifying the enemy as the antithesis of American values, saying, "We value life; the terrorists ruthlessly destroy it. We value education; the terrorists do not believe women should be educated or should have health care, or should leave their homes. We value the right to speak our minds; for the terrorists, free expression can be grounds for execution."

> *Citizens who want to be true Americans must continue to speak openly, associate freely, assemble often, dissent freely and protect their privacy.*

Once again peace groups sought to harness hegemony by associating dissent with the national principles articulated by the President. They saw Bush's policies actually limiting rather than upholding traditional American freedoms, and they insisted that the job of the true patriot was to protect the Bill of Rights. The AFSC enumerated a long list of constitutional rights whose use would form a bulwark against the new dangers facing the U.S., concluding, "Working in your communities to use and protect these rights in the weeks ahead will guarantee that terrorism has not destroyed the fabric of liberty or undercut our Constitution."

The point of such statements was not to engage in remedial

civics lessons with a public whose allegiance to America was clearly uncontested. Instead, these organizations contested something else—the actual meaning of national allegiance in a post-9/11 world, where much is thought to have changed. Recalling what they see as the original definition of a patriot, they argue that citizens who want to be true Americans must continue to speak openly, associate freely, assemble often, dissent freely and protect their privacy. As far as the War Resisters' League was concerned, this applied to members of the armed forces as well: "We encourage members of the armed forces to consider carefully their own role in a war which, despite its wide popular support at the moment, is a violation of our own constitution and of the charter of the United Nations."

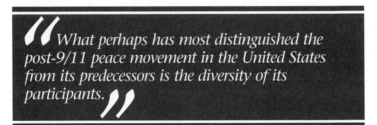

What perhaps has most distinguished the post-9/11 peace movement in the United States from its predecessors is the diversity of its participants.

Harnessing hegemony shifts the critical spotlight, holding power elites accountable to the same values that they reference to bolster their legitimacy. The AFSC invoked foundational American principles to challenge the government's policies: "The very principles on which this country was founded do not support the erosion of civil liberties or the . . . discrimination of entire groups of people for individual actions." The Women's International League for Peace and Freedom argued that the war in Afghanistan will not only make Americans less safe in the long run, but it will also destroy civil liberties and democracy, those values Americans hold most dear, and which are the United States' "greatest gift" to the world.

Commitment to tolerance, social equality, and democracy

In addition to calling for the protection of civil liberties, peace groups also appealed to Americans' commitment to tolerance, social equality and democracy. While addressing the scapegoating of immigrants of color that the September 11 attacks had unleashed in the country, FOR asked rhetorically, "Will we determine to carry out special acts of kindness by reaching across lines of difference with goodwill and compassion? Will we seek to overcome evil with good?" The Black Radical Congress associated anti-racism with true Americanism and with personal risk-taking on behalf of those threatened: "True anti-racism may require us to put ourselves at risk physically in order to defend Arabs and Muslims from unwarranted attacks."

Using victims of 9/11

Putting oneself at risk on behalf of others became an important touchpoint for rousing nationalism in post-9/11 America. For the media, the government and society in general, those who lost their lives in the bombings became symbols of a besieged nation. Politicians and White House spokespersons repeatedly referenced the victims in association with the administration's plans for war. In his first speech after the attacks, President Bush pledged to carry the police badge of an officer who died at the World Trade Center. In this charged political context, those who challenged the plans for a global War on Terrorism were not only deemed traitorous to the nation, but also callous and unsympathetic to the suffering of America's innocent civilians. This discursive turn of events created unique challenges for a peace movement already laboring under difficult conditions. How did the peace movement respond to the use of victims and heroes of 9/11 to promote militarism and war?

Peace groups began by immediately making clear their sympathy for the victims. For instance this compassion and sense of commonality was voiced by WAND: "We are deeply shaken by the horror inflicted on our country yesterday. . . . Like the rest of the world, we searched for hope and assurances of the safety of loved ones. Our deepest sympathy and our prayers are with the victims, their families, and the emergency response teams." Within days peace groups uniformly condemned the attacks, making statements such as: "The Black Radical Congress (BRC) strongly condemns the horrific terror attacks which occurred on September 11th, 2001. The brazen murder of countless thousands of civilians cannot be supported or condoned." In the process, peace activists discursively insulated themselves from allegations of being unpatriotic.

Peace groups also linked themselves to the heroism of firefighters and police officers who risked and lost their lives in desperate efforts to save others. For example, calling the actions of the emergency workers examples of the country's "finest hour," Pax Christi expanded traditional notions of both heroism and of nationalism centered on the defeat of opponents on the battlefield to include heroes who sacrifice to save and protect lives, at the expense of only themselves:

> We have witnessed countless acts of heroic self-sacrifice, love and compassion for those caught up in this tragedy. A new kind of American hero has been forged in the sweat and blood of countless fire fighters, police officers, emergency workers, doctors, nurses and volunteers who gave all they had, including their lives, for the sake of others. And in those instances when the ugly face of racism showed itself, countless numbers of people of faith stood in the breach and offered protection for our Arab neighbors. In many respects this has been our finest hour.

This image of the 9/11 hero was further put forth by Pax Christi as a "parable" by which Americans could live their lives and conduct their domestic and foreign policy, "preventing further victims, attending to vulnerable ones, sheltering from harm."

Harness or challenge hegemony

The attacks of September 11, 2001, challenged peace activists seeking to open space for critical analysis. As PMOs accommodated the political climate and used discussions of patriotism to call for peace, the question remained—was the peace movement better off harnessing hegemony or directly challenging it? On the one hand, social movements' research suggest that during low ebbs in levels of protest within a society, mass movements are not likely to form unless organizers can discursively tap into widely and deeply resonant identities, beliefs and values. Statements that directly challenge resonant cultural materials (for example, that racism and capitalism constitute the driving forces behind U.S. government policies) are unlikely to attract participants beyond those already convinced.

What perhaps has most distinguished the post-9/11 peace movement in the United States from its predecessors is the diversity of its participants. In recent anti-war demonstrations, people from all walks of life came to their first protest. The U.S. Civil Rights Movement amply demonstrated that demanding a state's policies to truly reflect the principles that underpin its legitimacy places enormous moral pressure upon the state to respond. We have also seen evidence that, in the post-9/11 context, harnessing hegemony not only insulated peace activists from censure and repression, but also has promoted dialogue. For instance, on one college campus, towards the end of official hostilities with Iraq, ROTC (Reserve Officer Training Corps) cadets and associated fraternities decided to hold a "Proud to be an American Day." The event offered both free hot dogs and live rock music. Sitting in the thick of things, two students held a poster that simply read, "Peace is Patriotic." When asked, neither of the students reported being intimidated or threatened. Rather they said that several people approached them to discuss what the war was about and what would happen next.

Quality is more important than quantity

Those who favor challenging hegemony argue that the quality of peace activism matters more than its quantity. If one assumes that the U.S. political system is corporate dominated and, therefore, largely beyond the influence of ordinary citizens engaged in low-risk activism, then building a mass movement may be less effective than organizing a committed cadre of activists willing to incur high personal costs to raise the costs of war to the state.

In addition, one might wonder whether harnessing hegemony ultimately reproduces existing power relations. In the context of the peace movement, nationalism contributes to war by devaluing the lives and rights of those who are not part of the nation. By feeding into the logic of nationalism, efforts to reconstruct nationalist identities may be counter-productive. Moreover, by failing to challenge capitalism, racism and patriarchy, appeals to patriotism simply divert attention away from the underlying sources of militarism, possibly limiting the transformational potential of social movements.

Proponents of harnessing hegemony counter that the staple materials of mainstream political culture are flexible enough to be combined in ways that offer poignant and systematic critiques of existing power relations. For instance, the principle of democracy can be enlisted in cogent critiques of capitalism, racism, patriarchy and militarism. Moreover, the love of one's nation is not inherently incompatible, with respect for and even identification with others beyond the nation. In fact, some of the peace groups studied constructed the "good American" in terms of cooperation with other states and respect for international law, enlisting democracy, civil liberties, tolerance and social equality on behalf of the cause.

Resilience of peace movement organizations is impressive

Whether to harness, or challenge, or attempt to combine both strategies will result in a global shift towards peace and justice remains an open question, which only history will solve. But the resilience of PMOs to adapt to U.S. culture in the post-9/11 context is both striking and impressive, even if it did not bring an end to all support for military might. What our data reveals is that in recognizing the shifts in the political landscape, peace groups in the months following the attacks of September 11, 2001, sought to create political and cultural space for opposition to war by avidly claiming ownership of an American identity and patriotic goals.

Each organization we studied condemned the terrorist attacks, but then used the shift in the American psyche to invoke a deeper discussion of what it means to be patriotic and what defines the core of American identity. Truth, social justice, compassion, democracy and an unswerving belief in the need for dissent emerged as the critical characteristics that these organizations identified as the backbone of being American. Thus the protection of civil liberties, opposition to unjustified military retaliation, and the affirmation of U.S. membership in the world community were for the moment transformed into definably patriotic acts.

7

The Peace Movement Is Threatened by Political Repression

Alisa Solomon

Alisa Solomon is a professor of English at Baruch College in New York, where she has served as director of the under-graduate journalism department. She has received several journalism awards and writes news features, cultural criticism, and essays for a variety of publications including the New York Times, Newsday, *and the* Los Angeles Times. *Solomon is a staff writer for the* Village Voice, *in which she has published hundreds of articles, including major investigations on immigrant detention.*

The public fear aroused following the September 11, 2001, terrorist attacks in the United States has led to political and cultural repression. This repression has been exacerbated by a powerful current of patriotic vigilantism that has spontaneous, threatening, and exaggerated reactions to peace protesters. For example, a former public defender was arrested in Santa Fe on charges of threatening the president and underwent five hours of interrogation because, in an Internet chat room, he had said, "Bush is out of control." When a woman at Yale University published an antiwar article in the campus paper, she received numerous rape and death threats. High school students have been punished for expressing antiwar views, and one university professor reported that the right-wing reactionism has given students the idea that it is useless and unsafe to dissent. Censorship has been further fueled by the prowar me-

Alisa Solomon, "The Big Chill," *The Nation*, vol. 276, June 2, 2003, p. 21. Copyright © 2003 by The Nation Magazine/The Nation Company, Inc. Reproduced by permission.

dia and by the silence of an intimidated Democratic Party that has offered no opposition to the prowar agenda. When the fundamental right and freedom of dissent is repressed, American democracy is threatened.

At a lecture in Cleveland in March [2003], Supreme Court Justice Antonin Scalia told the audience, "Most of the rights that you enjoy go way beyond what the Constitution requires." The government can legitimately scale back individual rights during wartime, he explained; since "the Constitution just sets minimums." For an increasing number of Americans, it seems, even such minimums are excessive. In August [2002], the Freedom Forum's annual First Amendment survey showed that 49 percent of those polled said the Amendment goes too far in the rights it guarantees, a ten-point jump since the last survey, conducted just before 9/11. In the wake of the recent war and the triumphalism that has followed, it's a fair guess that in this summer's [2003] survey, the numbers will climb even higher.

While we've seen a flood of antiwar activity over the past eight months, [before and after the Iraq war] we've also witnessed a powerful countercurrent of political repression. From shopping malls to cyberspace, Hollywood to the Ivy League, Americans have taken it upon themselves to stifle and shame those who question the legitimacy of the Administration or the war on Iraq. When we read a story here or there about the arrest of a man wearing a "Peace on Earth" T-shirt in an upstate New York mall, or about country music fans crushing Dixie Chicks CDs because the lead singer said she was ashamed of the President, each may seem like an anomalous episode. But taken as a whole, the far-flung incidents of bullying, silencing and even threats of violence reveal a political and cultural shift that recalls some of America's darkest days.

Freedom of speech repressed after 9/11

Like any avalanche, this one started at the top, and likely dates back to the moment after 9/11 when President Bush warned the world's nations, "Either you are with us or you are with the terrorists." From Bush on down, in the months that followed, government officials drew limits around acceptable speech. White House spokesperson Ari Fleischer told Americans to "watch what they say." Such words gained force when the Patriot Act gave the government extensive new powers to spy, interrogate and detain. When civil libertarians began to protest the curbing of constitutional rights, Attorney General John Ashcroft offered a forbidding rejoinder: "To those who scare peace-loving people with phantoms of lost liberty, my message is this: Your tactics only aid terrorists." These kinds of remarks from our government's top leaders, says Anthony Romero, executive director of the ACLU [American Civil Liberties Union], have granted ordinary people license "to shut down alternative views." The Administration has fashioned a domestic arm of its new doctrine of pre-emption.

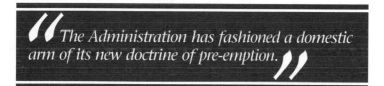

The Administration has fashioned a domestic arm of its new doctrine of pre-emption.

Rashes of American conformity and nativism have broken out before during periods of war, social strain and insecurity over national self-definition. During World War I, the McCarthy period[1] and the COINTELPRO [FBI counterintelligence] program of three decades ago, dissenters lost their jobs, went to jail and endured mob violence or government smears. Today's crackdowns do not match the force and scale of those shameful times, or take the same forms. History rarely repeats precisely those excesses, which have since been declared dishonorable or unconstitutional. Though Phil Donahue was recently fired for his views and charities have been canceling events with antiwar celebrities such as Susan Sarandon and Tim Robbins, the Hollywood blacklist itself, says historian Howard Zinn, could not happen again. Still, while the government expands its power even as it loosens constitutional limitations on it, the public acquiescence and participation—in suppression threatens American democracy anew.

Henry Foner, a longtime labor organizer who lost his state teaching license to the Red Scare, remembers the "tremendous terror" he felt in the McCarthy period, as "FBI agents were all over the place, visiting people's neighbors." Now, that fear is being experienced by Muslim and Arab immigrants, who are regarded as dangerous regardless of their political beliefs. Immi-

---

1. During the 1950s Senator Joseph McCarthy led a crusade to identify supposed Communists in government positions.

grant neighborhoods like Midwood, Brooklyn, home to more than 100,000 Pakistanis, have been decimated by the loss of thousands of men who were deported or who have fled. Many still languish in detention for minor visa violations or for donations to the wrong charity. Businesses have failed as customers have been afraid to venture out even to buy their groceries.

But if Arab and Muslim immigrants are enduring fear levels reminiscent of the McCarthy period, dissenters are experiencing a chill, according to historian Blanche Wiesen Cook, "more along the lines of the total repression during World War I, though we're not all the way there yet." The government has not revived, precisely, the Espionage Act of 1917, which barred from the mails any material . . . "advocating or urging treason, insurrection, or forcible resistance to any law of the United States"; or the Sedition Act of 1918, which outlawed virtually all criticism of the war and the government. Under that law, a man was sentenced to twenty years for stating in a private conversation that he hoped the "government goes to hell so it will be of no value." Today's clampdown, though far less systematic, is reminiscent: In February [2003] a former public defender, Andrew O'Conner, was arrested in Santa Fe for "threatening the president" and subjected to five hours of interrogation by special agents because he'd said, in an Internet chat room, "Bush is out of control." Glenda Gilmore, a professor of US history at Yale, sees significant parallels with that period, especially in the "nationalist hysteria that was in the streets and in the air." Egged on by government leaders warning of the presence of German spies and "seditious" antiwar labor activists, Americans joined mob actions to contain and castigate dissenters. Though not as widespread or as violent, patriotic vigilantism has broken out again across the nation. As before, it is often spontaneous, threatening and out of proportion to the action it means to challenge.

The new patriotism

During the First World War, a man was beaten by fellow baseball fans for failing to stand up for "The Star-Spangled Banner." Today's patriotic outbursts are less bloody, though just as emotionally intense. In the winter [of 2002/2003], hundreds of merchant marine cadets amassed at a Manhattanville College basketball game to chant "Leave our country!" at senior Toni Smith, who had quietly been turning her back during the national anthem all season. Practically every sports columnist and talk-radio host in the country made sure to get in his licks against the obscure Division III player.

At Wheaton College, a small liberal arts school in Norton, Massachusetts, seven housemates hung an upside-down "distress" flag on their campus house the day the war started. Their neighbors responded by throwing rocks through the students' windows, calling in death threats to their answering machine and strapping a dead fish to their front door, Godfather-style. Restaurants in town stopped serving kids from Wheaton, and bar patrons harassed them. Norton police recommended that for their own safety, the housemates move out for a few days. "I know it's nothing like Baghdad or Palestine," says Geoffrey Bickford, a recent political science graduate and resident of the house. "But being forced to flee from my home, having my voice silenced and living in fear because of my beliefs—that concept is so frightening."

Jingoistic broadcast media have provided Bush with his own 'protective league' by setting the tone for repression.

At Yale, when sophomore Katherine Lo also hung an upside-down flag out her window, several men wielding a 2 by 4 tried to enter her room late at night while Lo was home. They left a convoluted note on her door that ended, "F— Iraqi Saddam following f—s. I hate you, GO AMERICA."

In the swanky Detroit suburb of Birmingham, Shelli Weissberg recalls sitting down to lunch at a cafe with her 8-year-old daughter and one of the child's friends, when a man she'd never met stomped up and yelled at her for wearing a "No War" button in front of children. The Rev. Joseph Matoush, who led peace vigils in the military town of Twenty-nine Palms, California, found a letter tacked to his church door with caricatures of Saddam Hussein and Osama bin Laden next to the lines, "These are your friends! Why don't you leave America now."

In Albuquerque, humanities teacher Bill Nevins was suspended because, he told the local press, poetry students he coaches wrote and recited anti-Bush verses at a local slam. (School officials say it's because he failed to supervise the kids correctly.)

Students are punished for
expressing antiwar views

ACLU affiliates around the country report cases of students being punished for expressing antiwar views. In Louisville, Kentucky, Sarah Doyle and her two older brothers, inspired by ballplayer Toni Smith, decided to protest the War by staying seated through the daily Pledge of Allegiance. Doyle's seventh-grade teacher made her come up to the front of the room and recite the pledge twice; one of her brothers received in-school suspension. Bretton Barber, 16, was sent home from Dearborn High School in Michigan when he refused to remove a T-shirt labeling George Bush an international terrorist. "I thought it was obvious the T-shirt was protected speech," says Barber, who filed suit against Dearborn High in March. He says he hopes to "send the message that all high school students have the right to express themselves."

But as the social costs increase, how many people will make use of such rights? Tim Robbins told the National Press Club on April 15 [2003] that on a recent trip to Florida for an extended family reunion, "the most frightening thing . . . was the amount of times we were thanked for speaking out against the war. . . . 'Keep talking,' they said. 'I haven't been able to open my mouth.'"

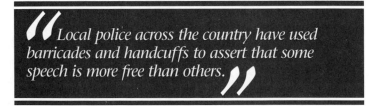

Local police across the country have used barricades and handcuffs to assert that some speech is more free than others.

A hush has even come over the arts, where free expression is supposed to be paramount. San Francisco's Alliance Française, a French language and cultural center, removed a sculpture that poked fun at the Bush Administration from its February [2003] exhibition. The Palestinian-American comedian Maysoon Zayid reports that clubs she plays regularly have taken to declaring certain material beyond the pale: No more jokes, for instance, about Ariel Sharon [prime minister of Israel] bragging to Saddam Hussein about the Security Council resolutions he's violated. In a joint act of self-censorship, New York's most established Off Broadway theater companies declined to participate in an April day of action called by the downtown group Theaters Against War. According to Mark Russell, executive director of the experimental performance space P.S. 122, people inside the National Endowment for the Arts have let it be known that "we shouldn't even bother to apply this year unless we have a really safe project."

This self-censorship extends all the way up to the halls of Congress, where Democrats have assured the President, in the words of Tom Lantos, the ranking Democrat on the House International Relations Committee, of "solid, unanimous support" in the war on terrorism. This silence on the part of the official opposition party serves as a restraining factor, too: Notes political historian Gerald Home, "Americans say to themselves, 'if people with money and power and influence are trimming their sails, why should little old me step forward?'"

A culture of fear

The September 11 terrorist attacks go a long way toward explaining why so much of the public has shivered quietly under this chill. "The fear in this country since 9/11," says Henry Foner, "is probably more intense than the fear of Communism in the 1950s." Already a nation primed to panic, thanks to sensational broadcast news and the Willie Horton tradition in political campaigns, a real attack on American soil profoundly shook most Americans. We've still not had a chance to recover.

Quite the contrary. Since the Department of Homeland Security began its color-coded alerts a little over a year ago [spring 2002], it has never designated the United States to be at less than yellow—at "significant" risk of terrorist attack. A shoe-bomber arrest, an orange alert for Christmas, checkpoints on highways and now a simulated bioterror attack in Seattle—a constant drumbeat reminds us of our vulnerability. Facing a shattered economy, the Bush Administration fans these anxieties, sending us to buy duct tape, warning us away from public monuments and scheduling the Republican Party's convention for New York City on the anniversary of 9/11. People who are afraid want to be protected and reassured, explains Barry Glassner, author of *The Culture of Fear*. When the White House tends to those fears by laying out a plan to protect Americans, however misdirected, people do not want to see those leaders undermined.

The events of 9/11 were destabilizing in another way: They forced on many Americans the astonishing recognition that their country is not universally beloved. While some Americans responded with teach-ins or protests, others have acted out aggressively—think of the 2 by 4, the broken windows, the angry outbursts—to quell the expression of these troubling doubts.

The anti-dissidents don't have to look far for validation—it's available every night from the broadcast media and most days from the halls of government. Fox's Bill O'Reilly criticizes progressive *Los Angeles Times* (and *Nation*) columnist Robert Scheer by hammering him as a "traitor"; defense adviser Richard Perle, objecting to a report on his conflicts of interest, calls Seymour Harsh "the closest thing American journalism has to a terrorist." When Tom Daschle lamented the President's failure to find a diplomatic solution in Iraq, it wasn't just Rush Limbaugh who laid into the Senate minority leader, but House Speaker Dennis Hastert too, saying Daschle came "mighty close" to giving "comfort" to the enemy. Joint Chiefs of Staff Chairman Richard Myers even lashed out angrily at former generals who had aired reservations about the war strategy, questioning their "agenda."

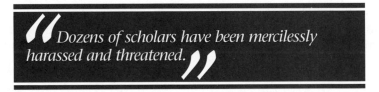

Dozens of scholars have been mercilessly harassed and threatened.

Woodrow Wilson officially sponsored vigilantism by forming the American Protective League, Citizen security forces that spied on and intimidated war critics. But then he didn't have Fox TV. Jingoistic broadcast media have provided Bush with his own "protective league" by setting the tone for repression. Who needs government censorship when stations owned by Clear Channel, the nation's largest radio chain (reaching, thanks to deregulation, 54 percent of all American adults under age 49), can drop the Dixie Chicks from their playlists, as they did in March? Clear Channel, facing a Congressional investigation into its business practices, promoted prowar rallies in cities throughout the country.

"Free-speech zones"

As an inflamed public, incited by government hawks and shock jocks, does its best to shut down critical speech, the state has used force to quash expression in the public square. Local police across the country have used barricades and handcuffs to assert that some speech is more free than others.

On October 24 [2002] Brett Bursey tucked a cardboard sign under his arm and headed out to the Columbia, South Carolina, airport, where President Bush was about to touch down and stump for local Republicans. But as soon as Bursey lifted his homemade NO WAR FOR OIL placard above the cheering throngs, police ordered him to leave the airport access road and take his message to a "free-speech zone" about a mile away.

When Bursey, director of the statewide Progressive Network, pointed out that people with pro-Bush banners were not being asked to move, an officer replied, "It's the content of your sign that is the problem." When Bursey refused to move, he was arrested and now faces federal charges carrying a potential penalty of six months in prison.

In St. Louis in January [2003], where Bush was giving a presentation on his economic stimulus plan, residents lined his motorcade with flags and signs. Banners proclaiming INSTEAD OF WAR, INVEST IN PEOPLE were selected by the police for removal; WE LOVE YOU, MR. PRESIDENT was allowed to stay. Police in other cities have subjected protesters to mass arrests, questions about their political views and affiliations, and even, in Oakland, rubber bullets. Legislation proposed in Oregon would jail street-blocking demonstrators as "terrorists" for at least twenty-five years.

Scholars are harassed

Just as the range of expression permitted in the public square is constricted, traditional "free-speech zones" such as campuses, find themselves under pressure to hold dissent in check as well. Middle East studies scholars have been targeted . . . in an aggressive, highly organized campaign attacking their positions not only on the war in Iraq but on the Israeli-Palestinian conflict. Campus Watch, launched in September [2002] to "monitor Middle East studies" on campus, has conducted virtual witch-hunts, posting "dossiers" on individual professors, distorting their criticisms of Israeli or US policy to malign them as "apologists for Palestinian and Islamist violence." In April [2003], Bush nominated Campus Watch founder Daniel Pipes to join the board of the United States Institute of Peace, a body designed to promote the peaceful resolution of international conflicts.

Dozens of scholars have been mercilessly harassed and

threatened. According to Amy Newhall, executive director of the Middle East Studies Association, some faculty members have had to abandon their e-mail addresses because they received so much anti-Arab hate e-mail—as many as 18,000 messages in a single day. Some have been "spoofed," meaning hackers sent out anti-Semitic diatribes from the professor's own e-mail accounts. Some have received menacing warnings— "Your neighbors have been alerted to your allegiance to Islamic terrorists"—and threats of violence.

No sooner had Yale's Glenda Gilmore published an antiwar op-ed in the campus paper than she received a rush of rape and death threats. It turned out that Andrew Sullivan [author and columnist] had set up a link from a blog denouncing her, and Pipes had attacked her in a hyperventilating op-ed titled "Professors Who Hate America."

In an article for *Academe*, Newhall notes that the purpose of these attacks is to stifle debate, and she warns that these efforts "will provide a model for future assaults."

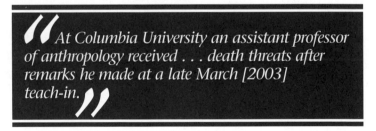

At Columbia University an assistant professor of anthropology received . . . death threats after remarks he made at a late March [2003] teach-in.

At Columbia University an assistant professor of anthropology received so many death threats after remarks he made at a late March [2003] teach-in that he had to move out of his home and teach under the protection of security guards. The professor, Nicholas de Genova, was quoted by *Newsday* as saying that he hoped Iraq would defeat the United States and that he wished for "a million Mogadishus." [Mogadishu is the capital of Somalia, where one of America's biggest military blunders occured.] An ugly statement, certainly, but not as extreme as Bill O'Reilly's enthusiastic on-air reading of an e-mail from a US Soldier who bragged, "You would not believe the carnage. Imagine your street where you live with body parts, knee deep, with hundreds of vehicles burning and the occupants inside." On O'Reilly's remarks? Silence. But dozens of news outlets, from the *Jerusalem Post* to CNN, seized on de Genova's, portraying them as a blood-curdling cry for American deaths. In an interview with *The*

Chronicle of Higher Education, de Genova said he had hoped to "contest . . . the notion that an effective strategy for the antiwar movement is to capitulate to the patriotic pro-war pressure that demands that one must affirm support for the troops."

The debate de Genova meant to provoke, needless to say, was never engaged. In an unprecedented move, 104 Republican members of Congress signed a letter to Columbia president Lee Bollinger demanding de Genova's ouster.

The defense mechanisms of democracy

Confronting the right's organized censure, and the popular patriotic flare-ups it inspires, it's easy to become demoralized. In the face of such effective pressure, says Gerald Home, young people like his students at the University of North Carolina—who were born during Reagan's presidency—easily learn to distrust the very idea of dissent out of a feeling that the right always wins. "They have a pragmatic, if not very deep, sentiment that's the political version of 'Nobody ever got fired for buying IBM': If you want to lead a comfortable, hassle-free life and not be a loser, be with the right," he says. "Unlike in the Vietnam period, we've all become sadly familiar with TINA—there is no alternative." In such a univocal world, dissent can seem downright futile.

As the space for dissent constricts, it's global public opinion and our own domestic civic institutions of liberal democracy—the courts, opposition parties, nongovernmental organizations and the media—that have to keep the channels open for alternatives to emerge. An inquisitive and vigorous press is essential, but too much of the mainstream media quickly succumbed to Pentagon spin. NBC fired Peter Arnett for making the obvious points to Iraqi television that war planners had "misjudged the determination of the Iraqi forces" and that there was "a growing challenge to President Bush about the conduct of the war." According to a leaked memo, MSNBC's sacking of Donahue in February [2003] was the result of fear that he might ask guests tough questions about foreign policy; he was replaced by right-wingers like former Republican Congressman Joe Scarborough. *San Francisco Chronicle* technology staff writer Henry Norr was fired in April [2003] after taking a sick day to participate in an antiwar protest, and two deejays at Colorado radio station KKCS were suspended in early May [of the same year] for playing a Dixie Chicks tune. Aaron McGruder's acerbic antiwar comic *The Boondocks* was dropped by the Boston Globe in late March when

McGruder penned a special antiwar "protest strip."

As for the courts, Ellen Schrecker, who has written several books about the McCarthy period, fears that they won't reverse their trade-off of rights for security the way they did some decades ago. By 1957, the Supreme Court had begun to rein in the most restrictive Red Scare laws. "They're feeble now," she says. "Twenty years of Reagan-Bush have really reconfigured the judiciary." The opposition party has also failed to rise to the occasion, leaving us, says Home, accidental anarchists, with "no electoral vehicle through which to express dissent." What we do have is a small but vibrant alternative press, growing numbers in organizations like the ACLU, more than a hundred city councils that have voted to condemn the Patriot Act or similar measures and an inchoate protest movement that thronged the streets all winter. Howard Zinn regards these outpourings as significant, "a broader shield of protection than we had during the McCarthy period."

What democracy looks like

One of the spirited chants at the February and March [2003] demonstrations went, "This is what democracy looks like." True enough, the multiracial, intergenerational demos, which brought together Plumbers for Peace and Queers Against War, corporate attorneys, public hospital nurses, students, retirees and Sunday school teachers, reflected the vast diversity and insistent expression of the American polls. But that can't be all that democracy looks like. It takes powerful civic institutions to provide checks and balances, meaningful enfranchisement and vigorous open debate to make democracy function. None other than Donald Rumsfeld made this point recently. He was talking about Iraq.

In at least one respect, the current situation has the potential to do graver damage than even the McCarthy and Wilson eras. Historically, civil liberties have sprung back to full force when hot or cold wars have ended, thanks in large part to the perseverance, or the resuscitation, of the press, the courts and the opposition party. But in an open-ended "war on terrorism," the day when danger passes may never come. Even if it does, the democratic muscle of the courts, the press and the opposition party—already failing so miserably to flex themselves— may be too atrophied to do the heavy lifting needed to restore our fundamental rights and freedoms.

8

Civil Disobedience Is Essential to the Peace Movement

Philip Berrigan, interviewed by Matthew Rothschild

Philip Berrigan was a Catholic priest who spent forty years of his life working as an antiwar activist. Berrigan wrote, lectured, taught extensively, and published six books, including Punishment for Peace, Prison Journals of a Priest Revolutionary, *and an autobiography,* Fighting the Lamb's War. *Berrigan was arrested over one hundred times and spent about eleven years in prison as a result of his antiwar activities. He died in December 2002. Matthew Rothschild is the editor and publisher of the* Progressive *magazine.*

All war is morally wrong, and citizens have a responsibility to confront and resist the U.S. government's propensity to wage war. The only way to effectively confront powerful forces for war is to break the law in the form of nonviolent resistance. Even Germany's Adolf Hitler may have been stopped using nonviolent resistance during World War II. However, an individual needs the support of a sympathetic community to provide the necessary strength and stimulus to continue nonviolent resistance activities.

Q: How many times have you been arrested?
Philip Berrigan: I don't know, well over a hundred, I guess.
Q: It's getting to be like an occupation.

Matthew Rothschild, "An Interview with Philip Berrigan," *The Progressive*, vol. 67, February 2003, p. 15. Copyright © 2003 by The Progressive, Inc. Reproduced by permission.

Berrigan: It's a necessity, it's an imperative.

Q: Why?

Berrigan: Because the only way you can get at the state is by dealing with its laws. That's why [American naturalist and writer Henry David] Thoreau would say, "Dissent without resistance is consent." If you dissent without breaking the law then you are legitimizing the system that allows this kind of latitude. You have to break the law to touch the state.

Q: Do you break the law to be effective or to bear witness? That is, if you knew beforehand that breaking the law would have no appreciable effect on what the government does, would it still be imperative to break the law?

Berrigan: Yes, it would still be an imperative. I guess we do it for both reasons. You try to be a Christian, you try to come from that tradition of the Jewish prophets and then Christ and everything since. That becomes your handbook. "Witness" is the key word. You witness against the injustice, against the atrocity, against the heavy-handedness, and all the rest. We try to make a statement to other people, and we try to say it's your responsibility, too. You have a responsibility to confront the war games—the American killing machine.

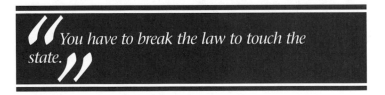

You have to break the law to touch the state.

Q: What do you mean by the war games and the war machine?

Berrigan: I mean what the Pentagon administers around the world. We have military bases all over the world, and that's purely to protect our portfolio abroad.

Q: Portfolio is an interesting word. Do you mean our investments?

Berrigan: Our investments, and our production, our exploitation of cheap labor and raw materials. We're on the scene to do that, and the military is there to see that it happens. The Pentagon is, admissibly, the most powerful institution in history.

Q: Were you opposed to World War II?

Berrigan: Not at all. I was a G.I., and I fought in Northern Europe. I was an infantry lieutenant. I was very much gung-ho, and I was a good young killer and only woke up later on.

Q: Was it a morally wrong war? Were you wrong to participate in it?

Berrigan: Very much so. Wrong to participate in all wars.

Opposed to all wars

Q: All wars?

Berrigan: Yes, all wars. That was total war. We lost seventy million dead through that war. If that's necessary to bring a monster like Hitler down, what more can be said about us?

Q: How do you respond to the question, "Well, if we didn't fight Hitler, he would be ruling the world right now and exterminating everyone?"

Berrigan: That's an assumption. There were all sorts of people who resisted Hitler nonviolently. The Norwegians did, the Swedes did. People all over Europe resisted Hitler nonviolently and did it without super loss of life.

Q: Were the protests against the Vietnam War pivotal for you in changing the way you acted in the world?

Berrigan: Something happened before that. I was teaching African American kids in a high school in New Orleans when the Cuban Missile Crisis started in October 1962. That was pivotal to me. It was Kennedy and Khrushchev debating as to whether we would live or die.

Q: Did you organize protests then?

Berrigan: I didn't realize I didn't know anything. I had a master's degree, I was thirty-seven years old, and I was an infant. A lot of friends helped me. I started to read, and to talk, and to seek out people who knew something, the Fellowship of Reconciliation, and then all of the civil rights groups.

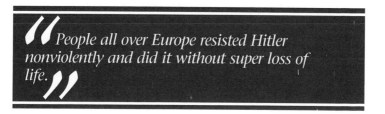

People all over Europe resisted Hitler nonviolently and did it without super loss of life.

Q: Tell me about Jonah House, the community you have in Baltimore.

Berrigan: We have seven adults there. We work with our hands. We do contract painting, roof work, masonry, carpentry, what have you—generally home rehabilitation stuff. We do a little speaking every now and then. We have a common purse. Nobody has any personal money, and we're accountable for what we spend. We live off of the cast-off food of society. We go to a huge produce terminal in Jessup, Maryland, and we pick over the garbage. We only use about 5 percent of that food for ourselves. The rest is shared in the neighborhood with the poor.

Q: Can you eat that way? It doesn't sound very appealing.

Berrigan: We eat beautifully.

Q: Why did you form this community?

Need for community support

Berrigan: It's something that we thrashed out after reading people like Gandhi and King and Thoreau and Emerson. We found that we could not stay in resistance unless we had a community. You need mutual support, the exchange of ideas. You need people to talk sense to you—you know, good people. You need all these things.

Q: Do you envision going back to prison to protest the war machine anytime soon?

Berrigan: Yes. If my health holds, I don't see any other course. I could stay out and take it easy or declare myself retired, but I'd be joining up if I did that. I'd be conscripted, and I would have agreed to the conscription.

9

Broad-Based Opposition to Permanent War Is Needed

Nonviolent Activist

The Nonviolent Activist *is the magazine of the War Resisters League. The league publishes the grassroots magazine as an educational tool to inform the public of pacifist issues, ideology, and activity.*

Members of the antiwar movement protest only during times of war or impending war. The antiwar movement is not enough to stop the permanent war movement present in the United States; instead, a permanent peace movement is needed. Peace movement activists must resist war not just with mass demonstrations but also with civil disobedience, refusal to pay taxes to support war, and counterrecruitment activities that would bring down the numbers of enlisted soldiers, making it impossible for the United States to wage war. Furthermore, peace movement workers must not only oppose war but the exploitation and political manipulation of occupied countries following war. In order to carry out all of these activities, the peace movement will need a broader base of support, one that embraces a wider cross section of the population.

Someone called the WRL [War Resisters League] office in mid-April [2003] about an upcoming demonstration and asked, "Are we protesting the war or the occupation?"

At that moment, it was a hard question to answer. It wasn't

The Nonviolent Activist, "The Peace Movement Between Wars: What Next?" www.warresisters.org, May/June 2003. Copyright © 2003 by the War Resisters League. Reproduced by permission.

clear whether the war was over. The United States seems to have entered into a permanent war mode, rather like that described in [British author George] Orwell's *1984*—or perhaps we should say, permanent attack mode: Even as [George W.] Bush & Co. mopped up in Iraq (that's "established the occupation," in Oldspeak), they appeared to be conducting a ghoulish casting call for the next war's enemy, with Syria and North Korea as the front-runners and Cuba as a sleeper candidate. Three issues ago, looking ahead to the war against Iraq and noting the unprecedented opposition to it, this magazine editorialized, "[The antiwar movement's] task now is not so much to change hearts and minds, but to build a diverse and credible movement that can mobilize voices and bodies. If we do that effectively, we can stop this invasion before it starts."

> *Opposing war is no longer enough; we need to oppose the misplaced priorities of occupation as well: the garrison building, the resource exploiting, the political manipulation.*

In retrospect, we have to give that prognostication a mixed review. The worldwide peace movement did succeed in mobilizing bodies beyond our wildest dreams: More than once, before the Iraq war had even started, millions of people across the globe spoke out simultaneously against it in the largest protests in history. Yet alas, we not only failed to stop it before it started, we failed to stop it before Bush and his craven coalition had finished devastating an already devastated country. Now, predictably, the numbers at the protests are dropping, although they'll probably rise again when the administration announces the winner of the next-foe audition.

Opposing the war is not enough

But permanent war is more than just country-hopping. We have to respond, not only to where the next invasion is, but to what the U.S. forces do when they're there. Opposing war is no longer enough; we need to oppose the misplaced priorities of occupation as well: the garrison building, the resource exploiting, the political manipulation. For all the administration's talk about protecting the people of Iraq, once there, all they protected was the oil. And the media, which were giving the opposition unprecedented visibility before the war began, in large measure relapsed into get-behind-the-President business as usual, leaving the cynicism and brutality of the occupation unchallenged. Thus, it falls to the peace movement to issue that challenge, audibly and visibly.

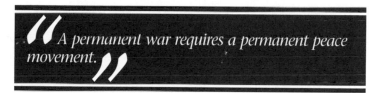

A permanent war requires a permanent peace movement.

A word here about which movement we're talking about: Historically, "antiwar movement" and "peace movement" have been used interchangeably. Strictly speaking, however, the peace movement—those groups that, like the War Resisters League, work before, during, after and between wars to promote the cause of peace in the world has always made up but a fraction of the opposition to any given war. Sometimes the fraction has been a large one, sometimes a minuscule one; few other than pacifists opposed World War II, for instance, while virtually all the United States left of dead center opposed the Vietnam War. But if there was ever a time when the cause of peace required that that fraction grow into a more substantial part of the whole, it's now. A mere antiwar movement will not be able to generate enough momentum to disrupt the stop-and-go rhythms of the permanent war; a permanent war requires a permanent peace movement.

Need more resistance

We also need to infuse our opposition with yet more actual resistance. Mass demonstrations against the next U.S. invasion are necessary, but won't be sufficient to stop it. Bush and his friends have made it eminently clear that they're not listening. They would have to listen, however, if enough people crowded the jails with civil disobedience, if not enough people paid war taxes to finance a war, if counter-recruiters brought the number of armed forces recruits to below armed forces sufficiency.

The last sentence, although clearly true on its face, begs the question, how much is "enough" to make them listen? That's easy: Enough is the number—unknown and unknowable in advance—that gets the job done. We don't know, for instance, how many war tax resisters it takes to stop war; but we'll know we've done the job when, in the words of the old poster, the Pentagon has to hold a bake sale to go to war. We don't know how many counter-recruiters it would take to whittle the armed forces down to numbers too low to accomplish the endless war's aims, but we'll know it when there aren't enough troops to mount an invasion.

But if that's going to happen, if the peace movement is going to be effective, it will have to be more broadly based than it has been in the past. No unarmed movement has ever succeeded without gaining the allegiance of a broad segment of the society it was trying to change—nor would we want ours to. As much as we want to end war, most of us also want to end it democratically, not by the fiat of a vanguard.

Need a large crew

In the end, that's the burden and the joy of pacifism—that what feminist pacifist Barbara Deming called the "exploration" that is nonviolence must be done in the company of the like-minded and the not-yet-quite like-minded. To face off against the largest war machine ever assembled on the face of the earth will require a large and motley crew bringing a range of gifts and perspectives to the effort.

We are calling, in other words, for both an escalation and a broadening of radical nonviolent resistance, which the War Resisters League has stood for for many years but which has never been more necessary than it is now. In the long-ago words of the great peace agitator A.J. Muste, "There is no way to peace. Peace is the way." Now it is the only way to stop the Bush permanent war.

10

The Peace Movement Should Be More Democratic

David Friedman

David Friedman is a mathematician, an educator, and a writer for Tikkun *magazine. He is an activist who has been involved in the anti–Vietnam War movement, the civil rights struggle, the labor movement, and the Berkeley Free Speech movement.*

Peace movement rallies in the United States before the 2003 Iraq war were supported by a leftist totalitarian group called the Workers World Party (WWP). The Workers World Party is a strongly anticapitalist sect that allies itself with dictatorial governments. Some peace activists have downplayed the involvement of the WWP in the peace movement in order to maintain the impression of a unified movement. Instead, American leftists in the peace movement must challenge antidemocratic ideas both inside and outside the movement and allow openness of dissent about peace movement leaders and their motives. Peace movement activists must advocate real democracy and reject totalitarianism.

Like many people who support the peace movement, I have found the politics of the mass mobilizations disturbing. The rallies are cheerleading sessions; they do not even try to reach out to the American people with ideas that can challenge American foreign policy, morally or intellectually. Many of the speeches have a mindless quality that repels the listener. The

David Friedman, "Democracy and the Peace Movement," *Tikkun*, vol. 18, May/June 2003, p. 40. Copyright © 2003 by the Institute for Labor and Mental Health. Reproduced by permission of *Tikkun*, a Bimonthly Jewish Critique of Politics, Culture & Society. www.tikkun.org.

speakers are loud in their denunciations of American and Israeli policy, but they lose moral force and political effectiveness by maintaining a tight-lipped silence about terrorism and dictatorship in the Middle East and elsewhere.

The reason for all this is clear to those who pay attention. The dominant force in the International ANSWER [Act Now to Stop War and End Racism] coalition is an obscure ideological sect, the Workers World Party [WWP], which leverages its mobilization skills to shape the message of the big demonstrations. I suggest interested parties go to their web site at www. internationalanswer.org and compare the long list of diverse endorsers with the short list of narrow-focus groups that make up the Steering Committee. A simple web search can tell you a lot about the politics of those who are running the show. Don't worry about the people who shout, like the Wizard of Oz, "Pay no attention to that man behind the curtain!"

Workers World Party

WWP has been around since 1959. They represent a brand of totalitarian leftism that defends the monstrous Slobodan Milosevic [former Serbian leader on trial for war crimes in August 2003], has not a word to say about Saddam Hussein, supported the slaughter of Chinese students in Tiananmen Square, and sided with hard-line Stalinists in the Soviet Union. Those of us who believe in peace and the reconciliation of peoples on a democratic basis cannot allow our voices to be muzzled by such as these. Their love affair with North Korea is as repugnant as our government's longstanding alliance with the Kingdom of Saudi Arabia and its prior relationship with the Taliban and with Saddam Hussein and his regime of killers and torturers.

TIKKUN Editor Rabbi Michael Lerner has been excoriated by some on the Left for daring to speak of this in the mainstream press rather than keeping the embarrassing information within "the family" according to some unwritten Mafia-like code of silence. Defenders of International ANSWER have attacked Lerner rather than responding to the charges that the politics of the mass mobilizations have been dumbed down and straitjacketed through ideological screening of the rally speakers. Their cry of "red-baiting" and McCarthyism is hypocritical since they are the ones suppressing dissent.

The coalition organizations attempted to defend themselves in a public statement declaring that Lerner was rejected as a speaker because he had criticized International ANSWER. They had an agreement, you see, to disallow rally speakers who criticized any of the organizing groups. For me, this "defense" was really a confession, exposing a complete lack of understanding of the need for diversity, debate, and criticism in the peace movement. It's not surprising that Lerner should be at the center of this uproar, since *TIKKUN* has always publicly raised issues that are considered taboo by most of the American Jewish establishment. *TIKKUN* readers know about the damage done to the political life of this country by those who seek to silence criticism of Israeli government policies and practices.

We challenge anti-democratic ideas when they come from George Bush and John Ashcroft. We must do the same when similar ideas emerge within the peace movement.

Everyone is for democracy

In the modern world, everyone rhetorically embraces democracy. The oil-man, George Bush, proclaims he will bring some phantasmagoric version of democracy to the Iraqis by bombing, invading and occupying their country. The same cynical use of words is displayed by anti-capitalist regimes like the Democratic People's Republic of Korea, whose very name is a lie. It is because democracy is a high aspiration of the peoples of the world that the term is used demagogically to enlist support for false causes.

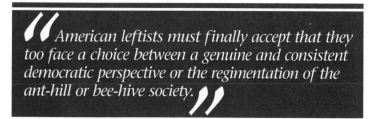

American leftists must finally accept that they too face a choice between a genuine and consistent democratic perspective or the regimentation of the ant-hill or bee-hive society.

How can we distinguish real commitment to democracy from the demagogic versions? In the final analysis it comes down to being informed, to knowing who is who and where people stand on important issues. Agreements to suppress criticism make the peace movement just as vulnerable to demagoguery and manipulation as the controlled mass media's one-sided stories make our society vulnerable to militarist propaganda.

For demagogues, democracy is not a principle, but a tool to

be used as a means toward power and abandoned when power is attained. Of course this is not a position anyone would proclaim openly. However, it has been a hallmark of the totalitarian left.

There have always been currents in the left that have embraced bureaucratic planning and the monolithic state, seeing themselves or their party as the embryo of a new ruling elite—ruling benevolently, of course, for who would dare to say otherwise in a police state? From this point of view, such leftists have opposed capitalism and its atrocities, thus putting on a "progressive" face, while defending authoritarian regimes and parties that are rivals of capitalism.

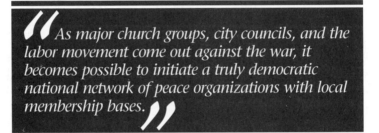

As major church groups, city councils, and the labor movement come out against the war, it becomes possible to initiate a truly democratic national network of peace organizations with local membership bases.

Pro-Soviet ideologues, including the founders of the WWP, are a classic example of this kind of totalitarian leftism.

They criticized Western capitalism while remaining silent about similar atrocities of their own patron states. It's a well-worn method: You don't defend the indefensible, you just keep quiet about it and attack the "other side."

The totalitarians spoke a populist language in countries like the United States, but where they achieved power every vestige of democracy was wiped out. Their true political nature was obscured by anti-capitalist formulas. The internal life of their organizations was manipulated from the top and brooked no dissent. Doris Lessing's brilliant novel, *The Golden Notebook*, reveals some of the flavor of that internal life as seen through the eyes of a weary and disillusioned participant.

The totalitarians were against war, except when their patrons went to war. Civil rights did not exist in their countries. They were pro-environment here, but said nothing as the Stalinist states ravaged the environment. People are still dying from the Chernobyl disaster [a 1986 explosion at a nuclear power plant in Ukraine]. They spoke abstractly of "the working class" while actual workers—denied the right to organize trade unions, to strike, to form political parties or vote in free elections—suffered the impoverishment and oppressive working conditions that go with powerlessness. In their ideology, nationalized property and the absence of capitalism were defined as progressive even though the benefits mostly went to a bureaucratic elite that ruled both the state and the economy through its one-party system and ruthless suppression of dissent.

Entire nations have suffered at the hands of authoritarian leftists. A heavy burden was placed on the human spirit. The price for pursuing a career or avoiding reprisals against families was conformity in political ideas, in the arts and literature, in every aspect of life. Silence about injustice was required, as was spying on friends and neighbors. Remember this history when you feel pressured to remain silent about misleadership in the peace movement.

Only a decade ago, a massive popular upheaval cast out the bureaucratic regimes of Eastern Europe and the former Soviet Union, and discredited their ideology. American leftists must finally accept that they too face a choice between a genuine and consistent democratic perspective or the regimentation of the ant-hill or bee-hive society. This is a political and moral choice.

A test of politics

Politics are tested in a crisis. Consider, as one of many examples, an article titled "Three phases of U.S. policy toward China" written by the Workers World Party's founder and leading theorist, Sam Marcy, during the 1989 democracy movement centered at Tiananmen Square. . . .

Marcy demands a crackdown on the students, but advises caution and the manipulative use of reforms until the Chinese government's actual repressive goals can be achieved. He baits the students for not being workers and peasants, even as he denounces actual workers supporting the democracy movement for "destroying the transportation systems" in several cities. It is standard practice for totalitarians to attack critics on spurious grounds, especially race and class.

Marcy rails against the reforms that were occurring in most of the "socialist" countries, except for the bastions of Cuba, North Korea, and East Germany. He remarks cynically that he wishes the Stalinist reformers were just faking it, "you know, a tactic agreed upon by the leadership that could change the next day . . . as was possible in the Stalin Period." Of course, the historical role of this Stalinist mode of operation has been to manipulate, disrupt, and destroy democratic movements.

We should take a moment to remember how unarmed demonstrators in Tiananmen Square were murdered—some crushed under the treads of armored personnel carriers, others beaten, arrested, and imprisoned.

For a new movement and a new politics

Today, we Americans on the Left face a time of crisis in our own country. The U.S. economy is in deep trouble, with massive bankruptcies and unemployment. Civil liberties are being undermined by the Patriot Act, arbitrary detentions, and a new, domestic security apparatus. American troops have been thrust into a dangerous and deeply unpopular war in Iraq while still fighting against guerrillas in Afghanistan. The Bush administration appears intent on an imperial Pax Americana based on U.S. military supremacy.

This crisis facing America has called forth the beginnings of a countervailing force—as yet unorganized and without a program or political voice of its own. Over the past several months the Iraq war and the Bush administration's assault on democracy have been widely debated throughout the country, and tens of millions of Americans have come to oppose the war. This is the true base of the peace movement. It is the reason hundreds of thousands of people have poured into the streets in demonstrations.

The central task of the peace movement is the organization of this mass base as a cohesive, democratic force with a positive social vision.

As major church groups, city councils, and the labor movement come out against the war, it becomes possible to initiate a truly democratic national network of peace organizations with local membership bases. The most immediate goal of this peace movement must be to put unrelenting pressure on the nation's political leaders, pledging to break with all politicians and parties that pursue war and abandon our democracy. At the same time, we must work towards and urge our leaders to embrace a new, democratic, foreign policy that can challenge the empire-builders and redefine the role of the United States as a genuine advocate of democracy and cooperation among nations. Nuclear disarmament must be demanded of all countries including the United States and its allies. The Campaign for Peace and Democracy has gathered thousands of signatures for a statement along these lines. . . .

This new foreign policy would be one element of a new politics based on the reconciliation of peoples in place of ethnic conflicts and economic rivalries. Such a political vision of global peace and democracy has long been advocated by *TIKKUN*. It is anathema to the totalitarian Left, which is all the more reason the rest of us should embrace it.

11

Celebrities Should Be Free to Express Their Antiwar Views

Erika Waak

Erika Waak is an editorial associate for the Humanist *magazine.*

The media were extremely critical of celebrities who spoke out against George W. Bush or the Iraq war, labeling them morally irresponsible and unpatriotic. Although antiwar celebrities encountered various amounts of criticism and repression from the media and others, many found their careers enhanced due to increased media attention. The media want it to appear that antiwar celebrities are suffering because of their activism in order to intimidate the general public into silence. Consequently, the Bush-friendly media are undermining the democratic principles of free speech and expression. When celebrities speak out against the war or the Bush administration's policies, they are helping to represent the voices of other celebrities, politicians, and others who feel too inhibited to express themselves in a hostile prowar environment.

The few celebrities who have boldly spoken out against the U.S. war on Iraq function as the only voice the Democratic Party has, since congressional democrats were mostly silent during the war. Perhaps politicians are wary of the extreme criticism that these celebrities have encountered from the U.S. media, which generally claims that those who stood in opposition

Erika Waak, "Celebrities Counter the War," *The Humanist*, vol. 63, July/August 2003, p. 20. Copyright © 2003 by the American Humanist Association. Reproduced by permission of the author.

to the war or President George W. Bush are morally irresponsible and unpatriotic. However, despite the media's attempts at portraying these celebrities as losing support and even receiving ridicule, media exposure has kept them in the public eye and stimulated curiosity. Moreover, sales of compact disks, books, and films of these dissenters have increased and changed careers for the better. And such "unpatriotic" celebrities are fulfilling a civic duty by representing those Americans who are too frightened to voice their own opposition but are speaking out with their dollars.

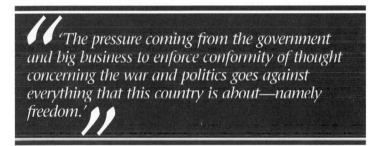

"The pressure coming from the government and big business to enforce conformity of thought concerning the war and politics goes against everything that this country is about—namely freedom."

Among the celebrities is Natalie Maines, a Texas native who is the lead singer of the country music trio, the Dixie Chicks. She stirred the most attention when she told the audience at a London, England, concert on March 10, 2003, "Just so you know, we're ashamed the president of the United States is from Texas." As a result, media with close ties to Bush reacted with a vengeance. The prime example is Clear Channel, a Texas-based monopolistic corporation and owner of more than 1,200 radio stations throughout the United States. Clear Channel promotes radio host Glenn Beck, an organizer of de facto pro-war rallies and hate campaigns against antiwar performers, including the Dixie Chicks.

Dixie Chicks doing well despite controversy

Because of this, the Dixie Chicks suffered a sharp drop in national radio airplay. According to the April 21, 2003, issue of the *Star*, one radio chain, Cumulus Media, even arranged for a tractor to crush Dixie Chicks CDs, tapes, and videos. Other organizations sponsored bonfires where their CDs were destroyed. This is a disconcerting reminder of cultural purges like historical book burnings and the destruction of the Iraqi national library, archives, and museums. Yet despite the controversy, the sales of Dixie Chicks CDs and concert tickets have increased. According to *USA Today*, as of April 24, 2003, the group's latest CD, *Home*, remains the top-selling album on the Billboard country chart—19 weeks at Number 1—and Number 30 on the pop chart. Their agent, Rob Light, told Billboard that week that, of their upcoming fifty-nine shows, only six had seats left and those were all 85 to 90 percent sold.

On the eve of their U.S. tour on April 24, 2003, the Dixie Chicks appeared on ABC's *Primetime Thursday* for an interview with Diane Sawyer. Maines said, "Am I sorry that I asked questions and that I just don't follow? No." She and the other band members—sisters Martie Maguire and Emily Robison—also told Sawyer that the consequences of Maines' comments were too harsh and that they've always supported U.S. troops, even though they question the U.S. war on Iraq. After receiving death threats, Maguire said, "I'm concerned about my safety. . . . At our concerts this year, we have to have metal detectors, and to me that's just crazy."

On the May 2, 2003, cover of *Entertainment Weekly*, the three Dixie Chicks appear naked under the headline "The Dixie Chicks Come Clean" with words such as "Boycott," "Traitors," "Proud Americans," and "Dixie Sluts" printed on their bodies. The *New York Post* reported Maguire as saying, "It's not about the nakedness. . . . It's about clothes getting in the way of labels." On his website, rock singer Bruce Springsteen defended the group's right to say what they believe:

> The Dixie Chicks have taken a big hit lately for exercising their basic right to express themselves. To me, they're terrific American artists expressing American values by using their American right to free speech. For them to be banished wholesale from radio stations, and even entire radio networks, for speaking out is un-American. The pressure coming from the government and big business to enforce conformity of thought concerning the war and politics goes against everything that this country is about—namely freedom.

Michael Moore's career rises

Another more political celebrity who has been shafted for his public opposition to the U.S. war on Iraq—and has subsequently experienced a rise in his career as a documentary film director and writer—is Michael Moore. At the seventy-fifth annual Academy Awards ceremony on March 23, 2003, Moore received an Oscar for his documentary, *Bowling for Columbine*, which attempts to answer why American culture is steeped in gun violence and fear. Upon receiving the award, Moore said:

> We live in a time where fictitious election results give us a fictitious president. We are now fighting a war for fictitious reasons. Whether it's the fiction of duct tape or the fictitious "Orange Alerts," we are against this war, Mr. Bush. Shame on you, Mr. Bush, shame on you. And, whenever you've got the pope and the Dixie Chicks against you, your time is up.

Although Moore received a combination of cheers and boos from the audience, he says on his website that, on the day following his opinionated speech, attendance to see the documentary increased 110 percent in theaters around the United States. In a week, the box office gross was up 73 percent, and *Bowling for Columbine* is now the longest-running consecutive commercial release in the United States. More copies of his video were pre-ordered on Amazon.com than *Chicago*, the Oscar winner for best picture. Moore's 2001 book, *Stupid White Men*, again became number one on the *New York Times* bestseller list on April 6, 2003. In addition, his website received ten to twenty million hits a day and, on one occasion, even surpassed the number of hits received by the White House.

The administration uses fear to manipulate the public into being docile and complacent so they do what they're told, sitting in mute opposition and fear.

So why does the media portray celebrities who oppose the war as suffering for their "wrongdoing"? Moore says that the media does this to make sure that those who disagree with the Bush administration remain silent. He says the media's ploy is to falsely say that celebrities are suffering for their dissent, for they are simultaneously sending the fabricated message that, of course, all American citizens who dare to do likewise will suffer. The administration uses fear to manipulate the public into being docile and complacent so they do what they're told, sitting in mute opposition and fear.

This manipulation of Americans through fear is precisely what Moore's documentary seeks to unveil. As he points out, those at the Academy Awards ceremony were cheering for a film that explicitly shows that Americans are violent—they're killing one another and citizens of countries around the world. The film indicates how the government uses fear and the media to quiet American opposition and makes them do as they're told. Moore says his film reveals that:

> The first Gulf War was an attempt to reinstall the dictator of Kuwait; Saddam Hussein was armed with weapons from the United States; and the American government is responsible for the deaths of a half-million children in Iraq over the past decade through its sanctions and bombing.

He says that the real purpose of the U.S. war on Iraq was for Bush to declare to the rest of the world, "Don't Mess with Texas—If You Got What We Want, We're Coming to Get It!"

Political activist Hollywood couple

Susan Sarandon and Tim Robbins, the political activist and Hollywood heavyweight couple, have also received their share of recrimination. Self-declared humanist Sarandon was dropped as a keynote speaker at the United Way of Tampa Bay, Florida, conference on women's leadership after receiving complaints about her antiwar views. Her offense was that, when introducing the obituary segment of the Academy Awards show, she flashed a peace symbol with her fingers while walking on stage. She, Robbins, and the First Amendment were also disinvited to a fifteenth anniversary screening of the baseball movie *Bull Durham* at the National Baseball Hall of Fame. The Hall's president, a former press secretary of President Ronald Reagan, decided that Robbins' very presence might undermine the efforts of U.S. troops in Iraq.

The April 22, 2003, issue of the *Washington Post* reported that when Robbins was asked about possible career repercussions due to his antiwar stance, he said, "I just finished two films. . . . I don't believe there's fallout. If there was, I don't think anyone would say, 'We're not hiring you for political reasons.'" Robbins spoke at the National Press Club in Washington, D.C., on April 15, 2003, and said that he has a fierce belief in the guaranteed rights of the U.S. Constitution. He continued:

> In the nineteen months since 9-11, we have seen our democracy compromised by fear and hatred. Basic inalienable rights, due process, the sanctity of the home have been quickly compromised in a climate of fear. A unified American public has grown bitterly divided, and a world population that had profound sympathy and support for us has grown contemptuous and distrustful, viewing us as we once viewed the Soviet Union—as a rogue state.

A wave of fear and paranoia

Robbins described a story his relative relayed about a local school board that decided to cancel a civics event, including a moment of silence for the victims of the U.S. war on Iraq, because the children were praying for U.S. soldiers and Iraqi civilians. Another friend shared an incident about a Southern radio disk jockey who called for the murder of a prominent antiwar activist. And apparently even some celebrities have caught the same wave of fear and paranoia even though it's evident that others' careers have only benefited from their expression of antiwar sentiments. Robbins said that a famous rock musician thanked him for speaking out against the war, for he felt that he couldn't do the same. He feared the ramifications from Clear Channel, which promotes his concert appearances and owns most of the stations that play his music. Robbins also said that renowned journalist Helen Thomas asked White House Press Secretary Ari Fleischer whether the United States was in violation of the Geneva Convention for showing prisoners of war in Guantanamo Bay, Cuba, on television. As a consequence, she was banished to the back of the room and no longer called upon.

Robbins said that those who supported the U.S. war on Iraq don't want to see the impact on the nightly news—they prefer the news coverage to be sterile and remain an abstraction, as opposed to the more accurate news that the rest of the world watches. He criticized the lack of political opposition—namely the Democrats who haven't had the courage to speak out against the Bush administration. He pointed out the contradiction of the United States:

> In this time when a citizenry applauds the liberation of a country as it lives in fear of its own freedom, when people all over the country fear reprisal if they use their right to free speech, it is time to get angry. . . . The fate of discourse, the health of this republic, is in your hands, whether you [are] on the left or the right.

He concluded his speech with the reminder that Americans' inherent right to criticize and question their leaders is what makes them Americans, and to allow these rights to be taken away out of fear is admitting that democracy has been defeated.

An open letter to Bush

Actor Sean Penn, in a prewar effort to exercise his democratic rights, wrote an open letter to Bush, which ran as an advertisement in the *Washington Post* on October 18, 2002. Penn says that he doesn't believe in Bush's simplistic and inflammatory view of good and evil:

> Many of your actions to date and those proposed seem to violate every defining principle of this county over which you preside; intolerance of debate ("with us or against us"), marginalization of your critics, the promoting of fear through unsubstantiated rhetoric, manipulation of a quick comfort media, and the position of your administration's deconstruction of civil liberties all contradict the very core of the patriotism you claim.

Penn writes of the collateral damage of those killed in war and how Americans are being forced to abandon the lessons of history in favor of having complete and total faith in the administration. He says that Bush claims to defend Americans from fundamentalism abroad while hypocritically turning the United States into a fundamentalist nation through the loss of civil liberties, heightened presidential autonomy, and the belief that the United States' manifest destiny is to govern the world.

Penn also toured Baghdad, Iraq, before the war and was later thrown off of a movie project in a contract dispute. According to the *New York Times*, Penn claims in a lawsuit that he lost the role as a result of his antiwar stand and was victimized by a resurgence of "the dark era of Hollywood blacklisting." Of interest, however, is the fact that the film's producer, Steve Bing, is a major donor to the Democratic Party.

Experiences of well-known singers

Penn's former wife Madonna, singer and international diva, produced an antiwar video in January 2003 to promote her new album *American Life*, although she abruptly canceled it on March 31, 2003. When asked in a *Dateline* interview on April 29, 2003, why she decided not to release the video, she said that she was aware what happened to the Dixie Chicks and, shockingly, she didn't want to cause waves for Americans who seemed to be largely divided and unstable due to the U.S. war on Iraq. However, she didn't fear the decline in her record sales.

Another singer, activist Ani DiFranco, performed at a Clear Channel sponsored concert in Newark, New Jersey, which was threatened to be cancelled because she wanted to invite guests to speak out against the war. She daringly went ahead and invited those guests on stage anyway. The show wasn't cancelled, although Amy Goodman—the prizewinning WBAI reporter who introduced DiFranco—told the *Village Voice* April 2, 2003, "The security guards took antiwar leaflets out of my bag," confiscating them from others as well, and the operators "were constantly threatening to cut off the mic."

> *Those who supported the U.S. war on Iraq don't want to see the impact on the nightly news—they prefer the news coverage to be sterile and remain an abstraction.*

A moderately well-known celebrity, actress-comedian Janeane Garofalo, has become the object of a vicious e-mail and telephone campaign led by Citizens Against Celebrity Pundits that has effectively intimidated ABC into postponing her new sitcom, *Slice O'Life*. . . . According to the *Washington Post*, Garofalo said, "I knew when I started speaking out that it was going to be unpleasant, and I've taken my punches. But the positives have far outweighed the negatives." Just weeks after she extended her antiwar sentiments on news programs, she received several unsolicited offers for stage roles, speaking engagements, and standup gigs. Only now, after more than fifteen years of comedy acts, has she made America Online's "Comedians to Watch" list. She says, "Now I'm almost famous."

> *The most crucial lesson is that, in order to be members of a true democracy, all Americans—whether or not celebrities—must always feel free to voice their opinions.*

According to the April 30, 2003, issue of the *Progressive*, Garofalo has been active with Win Without War and appeared on CNN, *Crossfire, Fox News Sunday, Good Morning America, Inside Politics*, and MSNBC. She criticized the media for wasting Americans' time with celebrity bashing and said:

> You can book a guest you can respect or you can respect the guest you book. They love to pretend that if you are in entertainment, that's what defines you and you can't possibly have any knowledge of what's going on in the news. So you have grown adult anchors and media people who are literally acting like twelve year olds, saying, "You shut up. You don't know anything." Literally treating you with the contempt of a schoolyard bully.

Citizens Against Celebrity Pundits has also energetically campaigned against actor Martin Sheen, whose antiwar views led to his credit card commercial being canceled. He appeared at a Los Angeles, California, vigil with "Peace" plastered on duct tape over his mouth. The *New York Times* said, "If Mr. Sheen is encountering turbulence with network executives, it is probably not because of his views about the war, as he has insinuated, but because of the slippage in *West Wing* ratings."

Television coverage is restricted

Speaking of television coverage, producer Ed Gernon wanted to air, during the U.S. war on Iraq, a four-part miniseries on Hitler's rise to power, and told *TV Guide* magazine that the timing of the series was absolutely apt. According to the *Star*, Gernon said, "It basically boils down to an entire nation gripped by fear, who ultimately chose to give up their civil rights and plunged the whole nation into war. I can't think of a better time to examine this history than now." His opinion was entirely too strong for CBS's chief executive Lesley Moonves, who decided to sack [fire] him. Yet television viewers indicated what they most wanted to watch during the war. As Michael I. Niman points out in his April 24, 2003, article in *ArtVoice*, "According to the *Nation*, more people watched Comedy Central's *The Daily Show* (4 million) at the height of the war, than watched Rupert Murdcoch's *Fox News* (3.3 million). And why not—Comedy Central actually had better war coverage. Though, ironically, Fox's coverage was funnier."

Some celebrities chose to show their opposition to the U.S. war on Iraq silently, like international singer Shakira. Appearing in a Reebok shoe commercial, she holds two white tennis shoes that turn into white doves as the camera zooms out to show her standing in a vast peace symbol drawn on the sandy beach. However, many celebrities have opted to remain both verbally and physically silent—notably leftist actors Tom Hanks, Woody Harrelson, and Robin Williams—missing a prime opportunity to fire up their careers.

Nevertheless, in all this, the most crucial lesson is that, in order to be members of a true democracy, all Americans—whether or not celebrities—must always feel free to voice their opinions. Bush and his cronies at Clear Channel, Cumulus Media, and Citizens Against Celebrity Pundits shouldn't be allowed to sanitize the public voice so it sounds like a monolithic drone of unification. Americans need to give Bush a forceful reminder, "Don't Mess with U.S. Democracy."

Organizations to Contact

The editors have compiled the following list of organizations concerned with the issues debated in this book. The descriptions are derived from materials provided by the organizations. All have publications or information available for interested readers. The list was compiled on the date of publication of the present volume; names, addresses, phone and fax numbers, and e-mail addresses may change. Be aware that many organizations take several weeks or longer to respond to inquiries, so allow as much time as possible.

Cato Institute
1000 Massachusetts Ave. NW, Washington, DC 20001-5403
(202) 842-0200 • fax: (202) 842-3490
Web site: www.cato.org

The institute is a libertarian public policy research foundation dedicated to peace and limited government intervention in foreign affairs. It publishes numerous reports and periodicals, including *Policy Analysis* and *Cato Policy Review*, both of which discuss U.S. policy in regional conflicts.

International Action Center (IAC)
39 West Fourteenth St., Room 206, New York, NY 10011
(212) 633-6646 • fax: (212) 633-2889
e-mail: iacenter@iacenter.org • Web site: www.iacenter.org

The IAC was founded by former attorney general Ramsey Clark. Its members coordinate activism, information, and resistance to United States militarism, war, and corporate greed domestically and internationally. The Web site provides contacts for centers for activism, relevant links, and information and articles on current IAC activism.

Military Families Speak Out (MFSO)
PO Box 549, Jamaica Plain, MA 02130
(617) 522-9323
e-mail: mfso@mfso.org • Web site: www.mfso.org

MFSO is an organization of citizens opposed to war in Iraq who have relatives or loved ones in the military. The group has contacts with military families in the United States and worldwide. The site offers related letters, statements and articles as well as links to other antiwar groups.

Nuclear Age Peace Foundation (NAPF)
1187 Coast Village Rd. Suite 1, PMB 121, Santa Barbara, CA 93108-2794
(805) 965-3443 • fax: (805) 568-0466
Web site: www.wagingpeace.org

The NAPF was founded in 1982 and is a nonprofit, nonpartisan international education and advocacy organization made up of individuals and organizations worldwide. The NAPF educates the public about peace and works to abolish nuclear weapons worldwide, strengthen international law, use technology responsibly, and empower youth to create a more peaceful world. Its Web site offers a monthly e-newsletter, book reviews, articles, links to related Web sites, and a section designated to peace heroes.

Pax Christi
532 West Eighth St., Erie, PA 16502
(814) 453-4955 • fax: (814) 452-4784
e-mail: info@paxchristiusa.org • Web site: www.paxchristiusa.org

Pax Christi is a Catholic organization that strives to create peace in the world by rejecting war and every form of violence and domination. Pax Christi advocates honoring conscience, economic and social justice, and respecting creation. Pax Christi's publications include the *Catholic Peace Voice* and the *Organizer*. Articles from these publications as well as statements on various international issues including the war on Iraq are available on their Web site.

Peace Action
1100 Wayne Ave., Suite 1020, Silver Spring, MD 20910
(301) 565-4050 • fax: (301) 565-0850
Web site: www.peace-action.org

Peace Action is the nation's largest grassroots peace organization. It has mobilized for peace and disarmament for over forty years. The group supports a student peace action network on campuses across the United States which works to end violence caused by militarism in the United States and abroad. The site offers fact sheets, articles, and resources related to the organization's current activities.

Peace and Justice Studies Association (PJSA)
Evergreen State College, Mailstop: SEM 3127, Olympia, WA 98505
Web site: www.peacejusticestudies.org

The PJSA is a nonprofit organization founded in 2001 that provides leadership in peace, conflict, and justice studies within universities, colleges, and kindergarten through twelfth grade. It brings together teachers and grassroots activists to explore alternatives to violence, and publishes the *Peace Chronicle* newsletter. Other publications include *Peace and Change: A Journal of Peace and Conflict Resolution* and the *Global Directory of Peace and Conflict Resolution*. The Web site has a list of related links and online resources.

Peace Brigades International (PBI)
Unit 5, 89-93 Fonthill Rd., London, N4 3HT UK
44(0) 20-7561-9141 • fax: 44(0) 20-7281-3181
e-mail: info@peacebrigades.org • Web site: www.peacebrigades.org

PBI is a nongovernmental grassroots organization that promotes nonviolent conflict resolution and protection of human rights. PBI has regional offices around the world and, when invited, sends volunteers to assist in troubled areas. The Web site has information on jobs with PBI and how to become a volunteer. It offers reports, journal articles, and information on PBI projects.

Peace Studies Association (PSA)
Earlham College, Drawer 105, Richmond, IN 47374-4095
(765) 983-1386 • fax: (765) 983-1229
e-mail: psa@earlham.edu • Web site: www.earlham.edu

The PSA works to enhance the academic field of peace studies in higher education. It is an organization of individuals and of college and university academic programs for the study of peace, conflict, justice, and global security. PSA publications include the *Peace Studies Bulletin* and the *PSA Newsletter*.

Plowshare Peace and Justice Center
1402 Grandin Rd. # 203, PO Box 4367, Roanoke, VA 24015
(540) 985-0808 • fax: (540) 982-0614
e-mail: plowshare@plowshare.org • Web site: www.plowshare.org

The Plowshare Peace and Justice Center is an educational resource center that works to create a just world peace that honors the dignity of every human being. The center promotes peace by acting locally and globally through nonviolent means such as organizing peace rallies. Its goal is for all to have resources for the development of a meaningful life. The site offers information on events and other news sources, a newsletter, information on local organizations, and links to peace and justice sites worldwide.

Resource Center for Nonviolence (RCNV)
515 Broadway, Santa Cruz, CA 95060
(831) 423-1626 • fax: (831) 423-8716
e-mail: rcnv@rcnv.org • Web site: www.rcnv.org

The Resource Center for Nonviolence was founded in 1976 and promotes nonviolence as a force for personal and social change. The center provides speakers, workshops, leadership development, and nonviolence training programs and publishes the newsletter *Center Report* twice a year.

United for Peace and Justice (UFPJ)
PO Box 607, Times Square Station, New York, NY 10108
(212) 868-5545
Web site: www.unitedforpeace.org

UFPJ is a coalition of more than 650 local and national groups founded in the United States in October 2002. UFPJ opposes what it considers the U.S. government's policy of permanent warfare and empire building. The coalition is responsible for organizing the two largest demonstrations against the 2003 Iraq war. The Web site offers resources for organizing peace protests, lists of peace and justice groups, and upcoming peace and justice events.

U.S. Institute of Peace (USIP)
1200 Seventeenth St. NW, Washington, DC 20036
(202) 457-1700 • fax: (202) 429-6063
Web site: www.usip.org

The USIP is an independent, nonpartisan federal institution created by Congress whose board of directors is appointed by the president of the

United States. The organization promotes peaceful resolution of international conflicts and sponsors many programs including conferences, workshops, and education programs from high school through graduate school. It has Web-published papers and a database of grants and fellowships. Publications include a weekly electronic newsletter and a bimonthly newsletter called *Peace Watch*.

Veterans for Peace (VFP)
World Community Center, 438 North Skinker, St. Louis, MO 63130
(314) 725-6005 • fax: (314) 725-7103
Web site: www.veteransforpeace.org

VFP is a nonprofit educational and humanitarian organization of war veterans and others working for the abolishment of war. The Web site offers information on VFP projects, a list of relief agencies, press releases, related links, and a newsletter.

War Resisters League (WRL)
339 Lafayette St., New York, NY 10012
(212) 228-0450 • fax: (212) 228-6193
e-mail: wrl@warresisters.org • Web site: www.warresisters.org

The WRL is a part of the London-based War Resisters International founded in 1921 that has affiliates in thirty-two countries. WRL members believe that all war is criminal and work on education and peace activism. WRL organizes demonstrations, cooperates with other peace groups, and opposes conscription and all forms of militarism including ROTC. The WRL staff trains people in civil disobedience and war tax resistance. WRL publications include the *Nonviolent Activist, War Tax Resistance, Handbook for Nonviolent Action,* and *Organizer's Manual*.

Web Sites

Free Republic
www.freerepublic.com

Free Republic is an online gathering place for independent, grassroots conservatism.

Patriots for the Defense of America
http://defenseofamerica.org

This is the Web site of a nonpartisan citizens group founded in New York City following the attacks of September 11, 2001. The group believes that the United States is not doing enough for its self-defense and must take a stronger stand against terrorism.

Peace and Conflict
http://csf.colorado.edu/peace

Peace and Conflict operates as a guide to peace studies and conflict resolution including a peace studies discussion group.

PeaceJam
www.peacejam.org

PeaceJam is an international youth peace program in which Nobel Peace Prize laureates participate in peace education for youth.

Peacemakers Trust
www.peacemakers.ca/index.html

Peacemakers Trust is a Canadian organization dedicated to education and research in peace building and conflict resolution.

Students for Protecting America
www.studentsprotectingamerica.com

Students for Protecting America is comprised of Harvard law students dedicated to supporting efforts of the United States and its allies in fighting the war on terrorism. Members supported the military action against Iraq and support the USA PATRIOT Act.

Students United for America
www.columbia.edu

This Columbia University nonpartisan student activist group is devoted to promoting patriotism, unity, and diversity within the community.

United We Stand
http://people.brandeis.edu

This group provides an outlet for Brandeis University students to express support for American troops and for the ongoing war on terrorism. Members believe that the Iraq war was a necessary evil.

Win Without War
www.winwithoutwarus.org

Win Without War is a coalition of national organizations whose members believe that international cooperation and enforceable international law provide the greatest security for the United States and the world.

Bibliography

Books

Peter Ackerman   *A Force More Powerful.* New York: St. Martin's Press,
and Jack Duvall   2000.

Alice Ackermann   *Making Peace Prevail.* New York: Syracuse Univer-
                      sity Press, 2000.

Roger W. Axford   *A Peace of Mind.* Tempe, AZ: Enlightenment Press,
                      2001.

Steve Breyman   *Why Movements Matter: The West German Peace
                      Movement and U.S. Arms Control Policy.* Albany:
                      State University of New York Press, 2001.

Michael Brown and   *Costs of Conflict: Prevention and Cure in the Global
Richard Rosecrance,   Arena.* Lanham, MD: Rowman and Littlefield,
eds.   1999.

Noam Chomsky   *Rogue States: The Rule of Force in World Affairs.*
                      Cambridge, MA: South End Press, 2000.

Chester A. Crocker, ed. *Turbulent Peace.* Washington, DC: U.S. Institute of
                      Peace Press, 2001.

John Darby   *The Effects of Violence on Peace Processes.* Washing-
                      ton, DC: U.S. Institute of Peace Press, 2001.

Marianne Elliot   *The Long Road to Peace in Northern Ireland.* Liver-
                      pool, UK: Liverpool University Press, 2002.

John T. Fishel   *The Savage Wars of Peace: Toward a New Paradigm
                      of Peace Operations.* Boulder, CO: Westview Press,
                      1998.

Nicholas Gammer   *From Peacekeeping to Peacemaking.* Montreal,
                      Canada: McGill-Queen's University Press, 2001.

Joanne Gowa   *Ballots and Bullets.* Princeton, NJ: Princeton Uni-
                      versity Press, 1999.

Jeffrey Hopkins, ed. *The Art of Peace.* Ithaca, NY: Snow Lion, 2000.

Scott A. Hunt   *The Future of Peace: On the Frontlines with the
                      World's Great Peacemakers.* San Francisco: Harper
                      San Francisco, 2002.

Colleen E. Kelley and *Women Who Speak for Peace.* New York: Rowman
Anna L. Eblen, eds.   and Littlefield, 2002.

David Krieger and Daisaku Ikeda
Choose Hope: Your Role in Waging Peace in the Nuclear Age. Santa Monica, CA: Middleway Press, 2002.

Brian D. Lepard
Rethinking Humanitarian Intervention. University Park: Pennsylvania State University Press, 2002.

Daniel Lieberfeld
Talking with the Enemy. Westport, CT: Praeger, 1999.

Rita Manchanda, ed.
Women, War, and Peace in South Asia. New Delhi, India: Sage, 2001.

Robert S. McNamara and James G. Blight
Wilson's Ghost. New York: Public Affairs, 2001.

Rob McRae and Don Hubert, eds.
Human Security and the New Diplomacy. Montreal, Canada: McGill-Queen's University Press, 2001.

Fred Rose
Coalitions Across the Class Divide: Lessons from the Labor, Peace, and Environmental Movements. New York: Cornell University Press, 1999.

Arundhati Roy
Power Politics. Cambridge, MA: South End Press, 2001.

Paul C. Stern and Daniel Druckman
International Conflict Resolution. Washington, DC: National Academy Press, 2000.

Bill Sutherland and Matt Meyer
Guns and Gandhi in Africa. Trenton, NJ: Africa World Press, 2000.

Howard Zinn
Howard Zinn on War. New York: Seven Stories Press, 2001.

Periodicals

Barbara Amiel
"Answering My Critics," *Maclean's*, April, 2002.

Dan Andriacco
"Thou Dost Protest Too Much!" *U.S. Catholic*, October 2003.

M. Arsenault
"The Continental Divide," *Maclean's*, May 19, 2003.

Fred Barnes
"The Pathetic Peace Protesters," *Weekly Standard*, March 10, 2003.

Hattie Brown
"Prospect of U.S. War Against Iraq Stirs Student Activism," *Education Weekly*, February 12, 2003.

Arian Campo-Flores
"Giving Protest a Chance," *Newsweek*, February 3, 2003.

Noam Chomsky
"What Lies Ahead for Iraq and the Anti-War Movement?" *Canadian Dimension*, May/June 2003.

K. Clark
"No Time for Battle Fatigue," *U.S. Catholic*, June 2003.

Elizabeth M. Dick
"If I Want Peace, Why Aren't I Doing More?" *Newsweek*, April 7, 2003.

Elizabeth DiNovella	"Janeane Garafalo Interview," *Progressive*, May 2003.
Luis Enrique Eguren	"Expanding the Role of International Civilian Observers," *Peace News*, November 2000.
Barbara Epstein	"Notes on the Antiwar Movement," *Monthly Review*, July/August 2003.
Liza Featherstone	"The Road to Peace," *Nation*, April 14, 2003.
David Frum	"Unpatriotic Conservatives," *National Review*, April 7, 2003.
Victor Davis Hanson	"I Love Iraq, Bomb Texas," *Commentary*, December 2002.
Molly Ivins	"Proud of the Peace Movement," *Progressive*, April 2003.
Esther Kaplan	"A Hundred Peace Movements Bloom," *Nation*, January 6, 2003.
Deborah Kory	"Reflections on the Movement," *Tikkun*, March/April 2003.
John Leo	"Antiwar Mongering," *U.S. News & World Report*, April 7, 2003.
John Leo	"Taking It Off the Streets," *U.S. News & World Report*, May 12, 2003.
Ryan Lizza	"State of Peace," *New Republic*, March 10, 2003.
Alex Markels	"Peacenik," *Mother Jones*, May/June 2003.
Lance Morrow	"The Right to Wear T-Shirts," *Nation*, February 10, 2003.
Doug Moss	"Charade," *The Environmental Magazine*, May/June 2003.
National Catholic Reporter	"The Peace Enterprise Goes Global," March 28, 2003.
John Nichols	"Building Cities for Peace," *Nation*, March 31, 2003.
Anna Nussbaum	"Generation Why," *Commonweal*, April 2003.
Mark O'Keefe	"Antiwar Movement Stalled in Pews," *Christian Century*, May 3, 2003.
George Packer	"Smart-Mobbing the War," *New York Times*, March 9, 2003.
Christian Parenti	"Many Peaces, One War," *Nation*, November 10, 2003.
Bill Pennington	"Player's Protest over the Flag Divides Fans," *New York Times*, February 26, 2003.
Katha Pollitt	"War: What Is It Good For?" *Nation*, April 7, 2003.

Julie Polter	"Lament, Dissent, and Dancing: the Movement Needs a Good Mix Tape," *Sojourners*, May/June 2003.
Anna Quindlen	"The Sounds of Silence," *Newsweek*, April 21, 2003.
Matthew Rothschild	"Patriotic Threats," *Progressive*, May 2003.
V. Schultz	"Lessons for Children: Importance of Protests," *America*, June 9–16, 2003.
Stefan Simanowitz	"The Human Shield Movement's Attempt to Prevent War in Iraq," *Contemporary Review*, June 2003.
Rebecca Solnit	"A Very Big Tent," *Orion*, May/June 2003.
Joe Stork	"What Solidarity Requires," *Progressive*, January 2003.
Silja J.A. Talvi	"The Public Is the Enemy," *Nation*, May 12, 2003.
Max Teichmann	"Wars, Demonstrations, and Peace Movements: Memories and Observations," *National Observer*, Winter 2003.
Josh Tyangiel	"Voices of Outrage," *Time*, March 31, 2003.
Peter Vilbig	"The Fight for Peace," *New York Times Upfront*, March 23, 2003.
David Warmflash	"Pioneers in Space, Pioneers of Peace?" *Humanist*, May/June 2003.
James Q. Wilson and Karlyn Bowman	"Defining the 'Peace Party,'" *Public Interest*, Fall 2003.
Anthony Wilson-Smith	"Reason Beats Passion," *Maclean's*, April 14, 2003.
Howard Zinn	"A Chorus Against the War," *Progressive*, March 2003.

Index